D1262170

CORPORATE RECORD KEEPING MADE E-Z

by
Arnold S. Goldstein, J.D., LL.M., Ph.D.

E·Z LEGAL FORMS®

Deerfield Beach, Florida
www.e-zlegal.com

NOTICE:

THIS PRODUCT IS NOT INTENDED TO PROVIDE LEGAL ADVICE. IT CONTAINS GENERAL INFORMATION FOR EDUCATIONAL PURPOSES ONLY. PLEASE CONSULT AN ATTORNEY IN ALL LEGAL MATTERS. THIS PRODUCT WAS NOT PREPARED BY A PERSON LICENSED TO PRACTICE LAW IN THIS STATE.

Corporate Record Keeping Made E-Z™
Copyright 1999 E-Z Legal Forms, Inc.
Printed in the United States of America

E·Z LEGAL FORMS®

384 South Military Trail Deerfield Beach, FL 33442
Tel. 954-480-8933 Fax 954-480-8906
http://www.e-zlegal.com/
All rights reserved.
Distributed by E-Z Legal Forms, Inc.

1 2 3 4 5 6 7 8 9 10   CPC   R 10 9 8 7 6 5 4 3 2

This publication is designed to provide accurate and authoritative information in regard to subject matter covered. It is sold with the understanding that neither the publisher nor author is engaged in rendering legal, accounting, or other professional services. If legal advice or other expert assistance is required, the services of a competent professional should be sought. From: *A Declaration of Principles jointly adopted by a Committee of the American Bar Association and a Committee of Publishers.*

Title: Corporate Record Keeping Made E-Z
Written by Arnold S. Goldstein, J.D., LL.M., Ph.D.

Important Notice

Limited warranty and disclaimer

Copyright Notice

Money-back guarantee

Table of contents

How to use this guide

E-Z Legal's Made E-Z™ Guides can help you achieve an important legal objective conveniently, efficiently and economically. But it is important to properly use this guide if you are to avoid later difficulties.

◆ Carefully read all information, warnings and disclaimers concerning the legal forms in this guide. If after thorough examination you decide that you have circumstances that are not covered by the forms in this guide, or you do not feel confident about preparing your own documents, consult an attorney.

◆ Complete each blank on each legal form. Do not skip over inapplicable blanks or lines intended to be completed. If the blank is inapplicable, mark "N/A" or "None" or use a dash. This shows you have not overlooked the item.

◆ Always use pen or type on legal documents—never use pencil.

◆ Avoid erasures and "cross-outs" on final documents. Use photocopies of each document as worksheets, or as final copies. All documents submitted to the court must be printed on one side only.

◆ Correspondence forms may be reproduced on your own letterhead if you prefer.

◆ Whenever legal documents are to be executed by a partnership or corporation, the signatory should designate his or her title.

◆ It is important to remember that on legal contracts or agreements between parties all terms and conditions must be clearly stated. Provisions may not be enforceable unless in writing. All parties to the agreement should receive a copy.

◆ Instructions contained in this guide are for your benefit and protection, so follow them closely.

◆ You will find a glossary of useful terms at the end of this guide. Refer to this glossary if you encounter unfamiliar terms.

◆ Always keep legal documents in a safe place and in a location known to your spouse, family, personal representative or attorney.

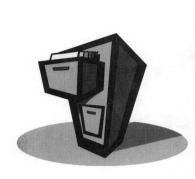

Introduction to Corporate Record Keeping Made E-Z™

Corporate Record Keeping Made E-Z contains all the important, ready-to-complete forms and documents you need to keep proper corporate minutes and records.

Virtually every corporate record keeping form is at your fingertips, giving you the protection you need without the inconvenience or cost of using an attorney for simple corporate matters you can easily handle yourself.

E-Z Legal Forms' Corporate Record Keeping Made E-Z is the ideal way to "get it in writing." What better way is there to legally document your important corporate transactions, avoid troublesome disputes, enforce your legal rights, comply with legal obligations and avoid liability?

Virtually every size and type of corporation can use Corporate Record Keeping Made E-Z. It can be used by both non-profit and profit corporations as well as by "S" corporations and regular "C" corporations. It will be particularly useful to small and mid-sized corporations which require less formal record keeping than larger, publicly owned corporations.

Written by a panel of attorneys and law professors, Corporate Record Keeping Made E-Z is considered safe and effective for use by non-lawyers.

FORM DIRECTORY

Forms by chapter

Chapter Two: Corporate organization

Chapter Three: Minutes of meetings

Chapter Four: Stockholder forms

Chapter Five: Operations

Chapter Six: Dividends

Chapter Seven: Compensation/Benefits

Forms alphabetically

-S-

-W-

How corporate record keeping can help

1

Chapter 1

How corporate record keeping can help

What you'll find in this chapter:

- ➡ Why corporate record keeping is important
- ➡ The corporate organization
- ➡ The role of the stockholder
- ➡ Running your corporation
- ➡ Keys to keeping good corporate records

Why good corporate records are essential

No business owner has become wealthy simply because he or she kept good corporate records. Yet, good corporate record keeping is essential for several important reasons.

1) **To protect you legally.** Generally, when you create a corporation, you create a legal entity separate and distinct from you as an individual. That means the corporation is responsible for its own actions. You are not legally responsible for the acts of the corporation, unless it engages in any criminal activity. That's why it's important for you to document all of the actions of the corporation. Without well-maintained corporate records, the courts may disregard your corporate status and allow creditors to sue you personally for

DEFINITION

debts of the business. This is called *piercing the corporate veil*. This means the courts can conclude that because the corporation did not accept its responsibilities and document its transactions, it is only a *sham*, or mere alter-ego of its owners. This problem occurs more often than you may think. This inevitably leads to personal as well as corporate liability for the business debts.

If your corporation has multiple stockholders, the need for detailed corporate records becomes even more critical. Any one stockholder may quite easily challenge the authority for a transaction. Only complete and accurate resolutions can demonstrate that the action was properly authorized by the stockholders and/or the directors.

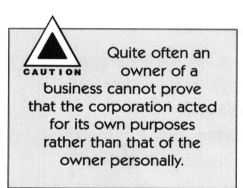
CAUTION Quite often an owner of a business cannot prove that the corporation acted for its own purposes rather than that of the owner personally.

A corporation can encounter many additional legal problems. Where transactions require director or stockholder approval, then a detailed record of the transaction as discussed and/or voted at a directors' or stockholders' meeting may resolve the dispute in your favor.

As an officer or director of a large corporation, you must particularly insist upon accurate minutes so you can prove your actions at these meetings and also show matters you voted against. Because lawsuits against directors are common, you must be able to defend your every action on behalf of the corporation. This is possible only with written proof, and that means good corporate records.

2) ***To gain important tax benefits.*** Have the corporate benefits you enjoy been properly voted? Have loans between you and your corporation been authorized in writing? Did you hold the required meetings to decide upon becoming an "S" Corporation or to change your corporation's fiscal year? Do you have resolutions authorizing your own salary?

The IRS will inspect your corporate minute book and without written documents to support the actions of the corporation, it may disallow any tax benefits resulting from those actions. This can produce a large tax liability—only because you failed to take the few moments necessary to keep up-to-date corporate minutes.

Don't you lose your valuable tax benefits. Make good corporate record keeping an essential part of your tax schedule.

note

The IRS is particularly demanding when it comes to corporate records.

The corporate organization

Corporate Record Keeping Made E-Z is the perfect way to keep good records of all corporate transactions—quickly, efficiently, inexpensively and professionally.

You can incorporate in any state, Puerto Rico or the District of Columbia, and much has been said about incorporating in corporate-friendly states like Delaware or Nevada. However, small corporations are advised to incorporate in the state where they are located and do business. If you do business across state lines, you may have to qualify as a "foreign corporation" in states other than your own.

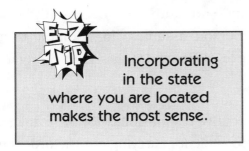

E-Z TIP

Incorporating in the state where you are located makes the most sense.

Once you have decided where to incorporate, a great deal of information about how to set up your corporation free or for minimal fees can be obtained from the Secretary of State of that state. Additionally, most states provide their own specific Certificate (or Articles) of Incorporation. Before filling out any incorporation records, contact your Secretary of State. A listing of the addresses and telephone numbers is found at the Resources section of this book.

Any corporation, whether large or small, conducts its affairs through three different groups:

- officers

- directors

- stockholders

Corporations, of course, also function through employees who carry out the day-to-day mandates of the officers. In most states one person may occupy all positions in the corporation (president, treasurer and secretary) and be its sole stockholder and director. Let's examine more closely the functions of each group.

Officers

Every corporation must have three officers:

- President

- Treasurer

- Secretary (or clerk)

As stated, one person may generally serve in all three capacities, although the person's responsibility and authority necessarily changes through the different offices the person assumes. In addition to these statutory offices, there may be vice presidents and/or assistant secretaries or clerks.

The president has the overall executive responsibility for the management of the corporation and is directly responsible for carrying out the orders of the board. The president may be elected by the board or by the stockholders. The bylaws prescribe this procedure.

The treasurer has a narrower role. The treasurer is the chief financial officer of the corporation and is responsible for controlling and recording its finances. Actual fiscal policy of the corporation may rest with the Board of Directors and be largely controlled by the president on a day-to-day basis.

The corporate secretary is responsible for maintaining the corporate records. This product derives its name *Corporate Record Keeping Made E-Z* from this office because it handles the role of keeping corporate records so effectively.

> *note* The authority of each officer is spelled out in the corporate bylaws and may be further defined by an employment contract or job description.

Directors

DEFINITION

The Board of Directors is the overall management body for the corporation. The board is responsible for establishing all business policies and for approving major contracts and undertakings. The board may also elect the president. Ordinary business practices of the corporation are carried out by the officers—and employees—under the directives and supervision of the directors.

The directors must act collectively for their votes and decisions to be valid. That's why directors act at a Board of Directors meeting. This, however, requires certain formalities. One is that the directors must be notified of a forthcoming meeting in a prescribed manner, although this can be waived or provided for in the corporation's Articles of Incorporation or Bylaws. A quorum is usually a majority of the directors then serving on the board; however, the bylaws may specify another minimum number or percentage.

Boards meet on a regular basis (monthly or quarterly), but in no case less than annually. These are the *regular* meetings. Boards may also call *special* meetings for matters that may arise between regular meetings. In addition, boards may call a special shareholders' meeting by adopting a resolution stating where and when the meeting is to be held and what business is to be transacted.

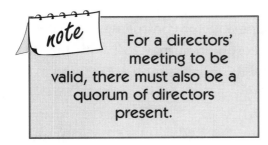

note For a directors' meeting to be valid, there must also be a quorum of directors present.

If your corporation is an existing one, use the resolutions contained in this book as a checklist to insure your corporation has satisfied all legal requirements.

Board members, like officers, have a fiduciary duty to act in the best interests of the corporation and cannot put their own interests ahead of the corporation's. The board must also act prudently and not negligently manage the affairs of the corporation. Finally, the board must make certain that it properly exercises its authority in managing the corporation and does not abrogate its responsibilities to others.

The board must be very careful to document that each board action was reasonable, lawful and in the best interests of the corporation. This is particularly true with matters involving compensation, dividends and dealings involving officers, directors and stockholders. The record—or minutes of the meeting—must include the arguments or statements to support the action and why it was proper.

note The first meeting of the Board of Directors is important because the bylaws, the corporate seal, stock certificates and record books are adopted.

Stockholders

Since the stockholders own the corporation, the officers and directors must ultimately serve their interests.

Still, this does not mean that stockholders are powerless concerning the affairs of their corporation.

Generally, the stockholders vote on the following matters:

◆ appointment of the president

◆ election of the Board of Directors

◆ major changes in the basic organization of the corporation. This may include:

- change of name or address

- change in the nature of business

- change in bylaws

- change in type and number of shares of stock issued

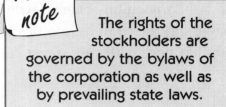

note The rights of the stockholders are governed by the bylaws of the corporation as well as by prevailing state laws.

- change in size or composition of board

- encumbering corporate assets

- dissolution or winding down of the corporation

- selling, consolidating or merging the corporation.

Stockholders, like directors, cannot act unilaterally. They must act either at a regular stockholders' meeting (ordinarily held annually after the end of the fiscal year) or at a special meeting of the stockholders (ordinarily called at the request of the board).

There must be notice of the meeting and notice of the agenda (items to be discussed and voted upon). Most states require 10 days' notice and not more than 50 or 60 days' notice be provided. You can specify a time period in the corporation's Articles of Incorporation. Waivers of notice are allowed if the Board fails to notify stockholders of the meeting or an emergency prevents adequate notice.

Stockholders may vote in person or vote by proxy, which means having another person vote in the stockholder's place. As with directors, there must also be a complete and accurate record—or minutes—of a stockholders' meeting.

Some states allow certain actions, e.g., amending the Articles of Incorporation, to be taken without holding a stockholders' meeting if (1) the corporation obtains a written consent to the action from the stockholders, and (2) the written consent states what action the stockholders have consented to. Check with your state to find out how many stockholders must sign a consent for it to be valid.

Occasionally, there will be a combined meeting of stockholders and directors. This is perfectly permissible, however, you still need complete minutes of meetings.

Running your corporation

Resolutions record the major decisions taken by the corporation's stockholders or Board of Directors. While not always required, it is a good idea to record your actions in the form of resolutions because they show outsiders that the actions were taken by and on behalf of the corporation. Some resolutions are passed only by the stockholders; others, only by the Board of Directors. Some must be passed by both bodies.

Remember that shareholders vote their shares and it is the number of shares—not the number of shareholders—that decide the vote.

Amendments to the Articles of Incorporation must then be filed with the Secretary of State in the state of incorporation for the amendments to become effective. Some states also require corporations to file a notarized affidavit, which verifies the number of outstanding shares at the time of the vote. Stockholders must also vote to dissolve the corporation or to file for bankruptcy or reorganization.

Resolutions adopted by the Board of Directors that generally do not require stockholder approval involve everyday operations of the corporation, including leasing, major purchases, hiring, banking, borrowing, investing, paying of dividends, salaries and bonuses, providing benefits for employees and changing the corporate status, such as obtaining "S" status.

 As a general rule all records, resolutions and minutes of your corporation should be kept in your corporate minute book for a period of no less than six

years. This is a good idea because sometimes a stockholder will want to inspect the corporate books and records to insure the corporation is being run in its best interests. We recommend that your corporation retain these records for a longer period should anyone ever challenge the actions of the Board.

note Any changes to the corporation's Articles of Incorporation or bylaws must be approved by both the stockholders and directors.

Corporate Record Keeping Made E-Z provides you with the tools necessary to meet all legal requirements. If properly utilized, it will provide all of the tax benefits and liability protection that a corporation affords you.

Corporate organization

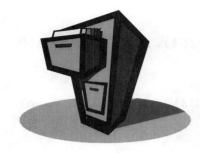

Chapter 2

Corporate organization

Forms in this chapter:

AFFIDAVIT VERIFYING NUMBER OF SHARES

AFFIDAVIT OF SECRETARY OF

_____

State of
County of

, being duly sworn, deposes and says:

   1. That I am the Secretary of   , a Corporation duly created, organized, and existing under and by virtue of the laws of the State of

      .

   2. That I am the custodian of the stock book of the said   .

   3. That the total number of shares of the capital stock of the said Corporation issued and outstanding on   ,   (year), is   shares, and that the persons whose signatures are affixed to the foregoing consent constitute the holders of more than a majority of the said capital stock so issued and outstanding.

                       _____
                       Secretary

State of
County of

   On   before me,   ,
personally appeared

                                             ,

who personally known to me (or proved to me on the basis of satisfactory evidence) to be the person(s) whose name(s) is/are subscribed to the within instrument and acknowledged to me that he/she/they executed the same in his/her/their authorized capacity(ies), and that by his/her/their signature(s) on the instrument the person(s), or the entity upon behalf of which the person(s) acted, executed the instrument.
WITNESS my hand and official seal.

Signature_____

My commission expires: Affiant _____Known _____Produced ID

                                          Type of ID _____

                                                   (Seal)

ASSIGNMENT OF ASSETS

TO

_____

BE IT KNOWN, for value received, the undersigned   of
                                    hereby unconditionally and irrevocably assigns and trans-
fers unto   of   all right, title and
interest in and to the following:

The undersigned fully warrants that it has full rights and authority to enter into this assignment and that the rights and benefits assigned hereunder are free and clear of any lien, encum-
brance, adverse claim or interest by any third party.

This assignment shall be binding upon and inure to the benefit of the parties, and their successors and assigns.

Signed this   day of   ,   (year).

_____   _____
Witness   Assignor

_____   _____
Witness   Assignee

BILL OF SALE

FOR VALUE RECEIVED, the undersigned

of _____ hereby sells and transfers unto

_____ of _____ (Buyer),

and its successors and assigns forever, the following described goods and chattels:

Seller warrants and represents that it has good title to said property, full authority to sell and transfer same and that said goods and chattels are being sold free and clear of all liens, encumbrances, liabilities and adverse claims, of every nature and description.

Seller further warrants that it shall fully defend, protect, indemnify and save harmless the Buyer and its lawful successors and assigns from any and all adverse claim, that may be made by any party against said goods.

It is provided, however, that Seller disclaims any implied warranty of condition, merchantability or fitness for a particular purpose. Said goods being sold in their present condition "as is" and "where is."

Signed this _____ day of _____ , _____ (year).

In the presence of:

_____   _____
Witness   Seller's Signature

                                                  _____
                                                  Seller's Address

BYLAWS
of

_____

adopted_____

BYLAWS

OF

_____

ARTICLE I: OFFICES

The principal office of the Corporation in the State of

shall be located in   , County of   . The

Corporation may have such other offices, either within or without the State of

, as the Board of Directors may designate or as the business of the Corporation may

require from time to time.

ARTICLE II: SHAREHOLDERS

SECTION 1. Annual Meeting. The annual meeting of the shareholders shall

be held on the   day in the month of   in each year, beginning with

the year   , at the hour of   .m., for the purpose of electing Directors and for

the transaction of such other business as may come before the meeting. If the day fixed for

the annual meeting shall be a legal holiday in the State of   , such

meeting shall be held on the next succeeding business day. If the election of Directors shall

not be held on the day designated herein for any annual meeting of the shareholders, or at

any adjournment thereof, the Board of Directors shall cause the election to be held at a

special meeting of the shareholders as soon thereafter as conveniently may be.

SECTION 2. Special Meetings. Special meetings of the shareholders, for any

purpose or purposes, unless otherwise prescribed by statute, may be called by the

President or by the Board of Directors, and shall be called by the President at the request of the holders of not less than   percent (%) of all the outstanding shares of the Corporation entitled to vote at the meeting.

SECTION 3. Place of Meeting. The Board of Directors may designate any place, either within or without the State of   , unless otherwise prescribed by statute, as the place of meeting for any annual meeting or for any special meeting. A waiver of notice signed by all shareholders entitled to vote at a meeting may designate any place, either within or without the State of   , unless otherwise prescribed by statute, as the place for the holding of such meeting. If no designation is made, the place of meeting shall be the principal office of the Corporation.

SECTION 4. Notice of Meeting. Written notice stating the place, day and hour of the meeting and, in case of a special meeting, the purpose or purposes for which the meeting is called, shall unless otherwise prescribed by statute, be delivered not less than (   )   nor more than (   )   days before the date of the meeting, to each shareholder of record entitled to vote at such meeting. If mailed, such notice shall be deemed to be delivered when deposited in the United States Mail, addressed to the shareholder at his address as it appears on the stock transfer books of the Corporation, with postage thereon prepaid.

SECTION 5. Closing of Transfer Books or Fixing of Record. For the purpose of determining shareholders entitled to notice of or to vote at any meeting of shareholders or any adjournment thereof, or shareholders entitled to receive payment of any dividend, or in order to make a determination of shareholders for any other proper purpose, the Board of Directors of the Corporation may provide that the stock transfer books shall be closed for a stated period, but not to exceed in any case fifty (50) days. If the stock transfer books shall be closed for the purpose of determining shareholders entitled to notice of or to shall be present or represented, any business may be transacted which might have been transacted at the meeting as originally noticed. The shareholders present at a duly organized meeting may continue to transact business until adjournment, notwithstanding the withdrawal of enough shareholders to leave less than a quorum.

SECTION 8. Proxies. At all meetings of shareholders, a shareholder may vote in person or by proxy executed in writing by the shareholder or by his or her duly authorized attorney-in-fact. Such proxy shall be filed with the secretary of the Corporation before or at the time of the meeting. A meeting of the Board of Directors may be had by means of a telephone conference or similar communications equipment by which all persons participating in the meeting can hear each other, and participation in a meeting under such circumstances shall constitute presence at the meeting.

SECTION 9. Voting of Shares. Each outstanding share entitled to vote shall be entitled to one vote upon each matter submitted to a vote at a meeting of shareholders.

SECTION 10. Voting of Shares by Certain Holders. Shares standing in the name of another corporation may be voted by such officer, agent or proxy as the Bylaws of such corporation may prescribe or, in the absence of such provision, as the Board of Directors of such corporation may determine.

Shares held by an administrator, executor, guardian or conservator may be voted by him either in person or by proxy, without a transfer of such shares into his name. Shares standing in the name of a trustee may be voted by him, either in person or by proxy, but no trustee shall be entitled to vote shares held by him without a transfer of such shares into his name.

Shares standing in the name of a receiver may be voted by such receiver, and shares held by or under the control of a receiver may be voted by such receiver without the vote at a meeting of shareholders, such books shall be closed for at least ( ) days immediately preceding such meeting. In lieu of closing the stock transfer books, the Board of Directors may fix in advance a date as the record date for any such determination of shareholders, such date in any case to be not more than ( ) days and, in case of a meeting of shareholders, not less than ( ) days, prior to the date on which the particular action requiring such determination of shareholders is to be taken. If the stock transfer books are not closed and no record date is fixed for the determination of shareholders entitled to notice of or to vote at a meeting of shareholders, or shareholders entitled to receive payment of a dividend, the date on which notice of the meeting is mailed or the date on which the resolution of the Board of Directors declaring such dividend is adopted, as the case may be, shall be the record date for such determination of shareholders. When a determination of shareholders entitled to vote at any meeting of shareholders has been made as provided in this section, such determination shall apply to any adjournment thereof.

SECTION 6. Voting Lists. The officer or agent having charge of the stock transfer books for shares of the corporation shall make a complete list of the shareholders entitled to vote at each meeting of shareholders or any adjournment thereof, arranged in alphabetical order, with the address of and the number of shares held by each. Such list shall be produced and kept open at the time and place of the meeting and shall be subject to the inspection of any shareholder during the whole time of the meeting for the purposes thereof.

SECTION 7. Quorum. A majority of the outstanding shares of the Corporation entitled to vote, represented in person or by proxy, shall constitute a quorum at a meeting of shareholders. If less than a majority of the outstanding shares are represented at a meeting, a majority of the shares so represented may adjourn the meeting from time to time without further notice. At such adjourned meeting at which a quorum transfer thereof into his name, if authority to do so be contained in an appropriate order of the court by which such receiver was appointed.

A shareholder whose shares are pledged shall be entitled to vote such shares until the shares have been transferred into the name of the pledgee, and thereafter the pledgee shall be entitled to vote the shares so transferred.

Shares of its own stock belonging to the Corporation shall not be voted directly or indirectly, at any meeting, and shall not be counted in determining the total number of outstanding shares at any given time.

SECTION 11. Informal Action by Shareholders. Unless otherwise provided by law, any action required to be taken at a meeting of the shareholders, or any other action which may be taken at a meeting of the shareholders, may be taken without a meeting if a consent in writing, setting forth the action so taken, shall be signed by all of the shareholders entitled to vote with respect to the subject matter thereof.

ARTICLE III: BOARD OF DIRECTORS

SECTION 1. General Powers. The business and affairs of the Corporation shall be managed by its Board of Directors.

SECTION 2. Number, Tenure and Qualifications. The number of directors of the Corporation shall be fixed by the Board of Directors, but in no event shall be less than (   ). Each director shall hold office until the next annual meeting of shareholders and until his successor shall have been elected and qualified.

SECTION 3. Regular Meetings. A regular meeting of the Board of Directors shall be held without other notice than this Bylaw immediately after, and at the same place as, the annual meeting of shareholders. The Board of Directors may provide, by resolution, the time and place for the holding of additional regular meetings without notice other than such resolution.

SECTION 4. Special Meetings. Special meetings of the Board of Directors may be called by or at the request of the President or any two directors. The person or persons authorized to call special meetings of the Board of Directors may fix the place for holding any special meeting of the Board of Directors called by them.

SECTION 5. Notice. Notice of any special meeting shall be given at least one (1) day previous thereto by written notice delivered personally or mailed to each director at his business address, or by telegram. If mailed, such notice shall be deemed to be delivered when deposited in the United States Mail so addressed, with postage thereon prepaid. If notice be given by telegram, such notice shall be deemed to be delivered when the telegram is delivered to the telegraph company. Any directors may waive notice of any meeting. The attendance of a director at a meeting shall constitute a waiver of notice of such meeting, except where a director attends a meeting for the express purpose of objecting to the transaction of any business because the meeting is not lawfully called or convened.

SECTION 6. Quorum. A majority of the number of directors fixed by Section 2 of this Article III shall constitute a quorum for the transaction of business at any meeting of the Board of Directors, but if less than such majority is present at a meeting, a majority of the directors present may adjourn the meeting from time to time without further notice.

SECTION 7. Manner of Acting. The act of the majority of the directors present at a meeting at which a quorum is present shall be the act of the Board of Directors.

SECTION 8. Action Without a Meeting. Any action that may be taken by the Board of Directors at a meeting may be taken without a meeting if a consent in writing, setting forth the action so to be taken, shall be signed before such action by all of the directors.

SECTION 9. Vacancies. Any vacancy occurring in the Board of Directors may be filled by the affirmative vote of a majority of the remaining directors though less than a quorum of the Board of Directors, unless otherwise provided by law. A director elected to fill a vacancy shall be elected for the unexpired term of his predecessor in office. Any directorship to be filled by reason of an increase in the number of directors may be filled by election by the Board of Directors for a term of office continuing only until the next election of directors by the shareholders.

SECTION 10. Compensation. By resolution of the Board of Directors, each director may be paid his expenses, if any, of attendance at each meeting of the Board of Directors, and may be paid a stated salary as a director or a fixed sum for attendance at each meeting of the Board of Directors or both. No such payment shall preclude any director from serving the Corporation in any other capacity and receiving compensation thereof.

SECTION 11. Presumption of Assent. A director of the Corporation who is present at a meeting of the Board of Directors at which action on any corporate matter is taken shall be presumed to have assented to the action taken unless his dissent shall be entered in the minutes of the meeting or unless he shall file his written dissent to such action with the person acting as the Secretary of the meeting before the adjournment thereof, or shall forward such dissent by registered mail to the Secretary of the Corporation immediately after the adjournment of the meeting. Such right to dissent shall not apply to a director who voted in favor of such action.

ARTICLE IV: OFFICERS

SECTION 1. Number. The officers of the Corporation shall be a President, one or more Vice Presidents, a Secretary and a Treasurer, each of whom shall be elected by the Board of Directors. Such other officers and assistant officers as may be deemed necessary may be elected or appointed by the Board of Directors, including a Chairman of the Board. In its discretion, the Board of Directors may leave unfilled for any such period as it may determine any office except those of President and Secretary. Any two or more offices may be held by the same person, except for the offices of President and Secretary which may not be held by the same person. Officers may be directors or shareholders of the Corporation.

SECTION 2. Election and Term of Office. The officers of the Corporation to be elected by the Board of Directors shall be elected annually by the Board of Directors at the first meeting of the Board of Directors held after each annual meeting of the shareholders. If the election of officers shall not be held at such meeting, such election shall be held as soon thereafter as conveniently may be. Each officer shall hold office until his successor shall have been duly elected and shall have qualified, or until his death, or until he shall resign or shall have been removed in the manner hereinafter provided.

SECTION 3. Removal. Any officer or agent may be removed by the Board of Directors whenever, in its judgment, the best interests of the Corporation will be served thereby, but such removal shall be without prejudice to the contract rights, if any, of the person so removed. Election or appointment of an officer or agent shall not of itself create contract rights, and such appointment shall be terminable at will.

SECTION 4. Vacancies. A vacancy in any office because of death, resignation, removal, disqualification or otherwise, may be filled by the Board of Directors for the unexpired portion of the term.

SECTION 5. President. The President shall be the principal executive officer of the Corporation and, subject to the control of the Board of Directors, shall in general supervise and control all of the business and affairs of the Corporation. He shall, when present, preside at all meetings of the shareholders and of the Board of Directors, unless there is a Chairman of the Board, in which case the Chairman shall preside. He may sign, with the Secretary or any other proper officer of the Corporation thereunto authorized by the Board of Directors, certificates for shares of the Corporation, any deeds, mortgages, bonds, contracts, or other instruments which the Board of Directors has authorized to be executed, except in cases where the signing and execution thereof shall be expressly delegated by the Board of Directors or by these Bylaws to some other officer or agent of the Corporation, or shall be required by law to be otherwise signed or executed; and in general shall perform all duties incident to the office of President and such other duties as may be prescribed by the Board of Directors from time to time.

SECTION 6. Vice President. In the absence of the president or in event of his death, inability or refusal to act, the Vice President shall perform the duties of the President, and when so acting, shall have all the powers of and be subject to all the restrictions upon the President. The Vice President shall perform such other duties as from time to time may be assigned to him by the President or by the Board of Directors. If there is more than one Vice President, each Vice President shall succeed to the duties of the President in order of rank as determined by the Board of Directors. If no such rank has been determined, then each Vice President shall succeed to the duties of the President in order of date of election, the earliest date having the first rank.

SECTION 7. Secretary. The Secretary shall: (a) keep the minutes of the proceedings of the shareholders and of the Board of Directors in one or more minute books provided for that purpose; (b) see that all notices are duly given in accordance with the provisions of these Bylaws or as required by law; (c) be custodian of the corporate records and of the seal of the Corporation and see that the seal of the Corporation is affixed to all documents, the execution of which on behalf of the Corporation under its seal is duly authorized; (d) keep a register of the post office address of each shareholder which shall be furnished to the Secretary by such shareholder; (e) sign with the President certificates for shares of the Corporation, the issuance of which shall have been authorized by resolution of the Board of Directors; (f) have general charge of the stock transfer books of the Corporation; and (g) in general perform all duties incident to the office of the Secretary and such other duties as from time to time may be assigned to him by the President or by the Board of Directors.

SECTION 8. Treasurer. The Treasurer shall: (a) have charge and custody of and be responsible for all funds and securities of the Corporation; (b) receive and give receipts for moneys due and payable to the Corporation from any source whatsoever, and deposit all such moneys in the name of the Corporation in such banks, trust companies or other depositories as shall be selected in accordance with the provisions of Article VI of these Bylaws; and (c) in general perform all of the duties incident to the office of Treasurer and such other duties as from time to time may be assigned to him by the President or by the Board of Directors. If required by the Board of Directors, the Treasurer shall give a bond for the faithful discharge of his duties in such sum and with such sureties as the Board of Directors shall determine.

SECTION 9. Salaries. The salaries of the officers shall be fixed from time to time by the Board of Directors, and no officer shall be prevented from receiving such salary by reason of the fact that he is also a director of the Corporation.

ARTICLE V: INDEMNITY

The Corporation shall indemnify its directors, officers and employees as follows:

(a) Every director, officer, or employee of the Corporation shall be indemnified by the Corporation against all expenses and liabilities, including counsel fees, reasonably incurred by or imposed upon him in connection with any proceeding to which he may become involved, by reason of his being or having been a director, officer, employee or agent of the Corporation or is or was serving at the request of the Corporation as a director, officer, employee or agent of the corporation, partnership, joint venture, trust or enterprise, or any settlement thereof, whether or not he is a director, officer, employee or agent at the time such expenses are incurred, except in such cases wherein the director, officer, or employee is adjudged guilty of willful misfeasance or malfeasance in the performance of his duties; provided that in the event of a settlement the indemnification herein shall apply only when the Board of Directors approves such settlement and reimbursement as being for the best interests of the Corporation.

(b) The Corporation shall provide to any person who is or was a director, officer, employee, or agent of the Corporation or is or was serving at the request of the Corporation as a director, officer, employee or agent of the corporation, partnership, joint venture, trust or enterprise, the indemnity against expenses of suit, litigation or other proceedings which is specifically permissible under applicable law.

(c) The Board of Directors may, in its discretion, direct the purchase of liability insurance by way of implementing the provisions of this Article V.

ARTICLE VI: CONTRACTS, LOANS, CHECKS AND DEPOSITS

SECTION 1. Contracts. The Board of Directors may authorize any officer or officers, agent or agents, to enter into any contract or execute and deliver any instrument in the name of and on behalf of the Corporation, and such authority may be general or confined to specific instances.

SECTION 2. Loans. No loans shall be contracted on behalf of the Corporation and no evidences of indebtedness shall be issued in its name unless authorized by a resolution of the Board of Directors. Such authority may be general or confined to specific instances.

SECTION 3. Checks, Drafts, etc. All checks, drafts or other orders for the payment of money, notes or other evidences of indebtedness issued in the name of the Corporation, shall be signed by such officer or officers, agent or agents of the Corporation and in such manner as shall from time to time be determined by resolution of the Board of Directors.

SECTION 4. Deposits. All funds of the Corporation not otherwise employed shall be deposited from time to time to the credit of the Corporation in such banks, trust companies or other depositories as the Board of Directors may select.

ARTICLE VII

CERTIFICATES FOR SHARES AND THEIR TRANSFER

SECTION 1. Certificates for Shares. Certificates representing shares of the Corporation shall be in such form as shall be determined by the Board of Directors. Such certificates shall be signed by the President and by the Secretary or by such other officers authorized by law and by the Board of Directors so to do, and sealed with the corporate seal. All certificates for shares shall be consecutively numbered or otherwise identified. The name and address of the person to whom the shares represented thereby are issued, with the number of shares and date of issue, shall be entered on the stock transfer books of the Corporation. All certificates surrendered to the Corporation for transfer shall be cancelled and no new certificate shall be issued until the former certificate for a like number of shares shall have been surrendered and cancelled, except that in case of a lost, destroyed or mutilated certificate a new one may be issued therefore upon such terms and indemnity to the Corporation as the Board of Directors may prescribe.

SECTION 2. Transfer of Shares. Transfer of shares of the Corporation shall be made only on the stock transfer books of the Corporation by the holder of record thereof or by his legal representative, who shall furnish proper evidence of authority to transfer, or by his attorney thereunto authorized by power of attorney duly executed and filed with the Secretary of the Corporation, and on surrender for cancellation of the certificate for such shares. The person in whose name shares stand on the books of the Corporation shall be deemed by the Corporation to be the owner thereof for all purposes. Provided, however, that upon any action undertaken by the shareholders to elect S Corporation status pursuant to Section 1362 of the Internal Revenue Code and upon any shareholders agreement thereto restricting the transfer of said shares so as to disqualify said S Corporation status, said restriction on transfer shall be made a part of the Bylaws so long as said agreement is in force and effect.

ARTICLE VIII: FISCAL YEAR

The fiscal year of the Corporation shall begin on the   day of   and end on the   day of   of each year.

ARTICLE IX: DIVIDENDS

The Board of Directors may from time to time declare, and the Corporation may pay, dividends on its outstanding shares in the manner and upon the terms and conditions provided by law and its Articles of Incorporation.

ARTICLE X: CORPORATE SEAL

The Board of Directors shall provide a corporate seal which shall be circular in form and shall have inscribed thereon the name of the Corporation and the state of incorporation and the words, *Corporate Seal*.

ARTICLE XI: WAIVER OF NOTICE

Unless otherwise provided by law, whenever any notice is required to be given to any shareholder or director of the Corporation under the provisions of these Bylaws or under the provisions of the Articles of Incorporation or under the provisions of the applicable Business Corporation Act, a waiver thereof in writing, signed by the person or persons entitled to such notice, whether before or after the time stated therein, shall be deemed equivalent to the giving of such notice.

ARTICLE XII: AMENDMENTS

These Bylaws may be altered, amended or repealed and new Bylaws may be adopted by the Board of Directors at any regular or special meeting of the Board of Directors.

The above Bylaws are certified to have been adopted by the Board of Directors of the Corporation on the   day of   ,   (year).

_____

Secretary

CERTIFICATE OF AMENDMENT

_____

, a corporation of the State of

whose registered office is located at

, certifies pursuant to the provisions of

, that at a meeting of the stockholders of said corporation called for the purpose of

amending the Articles of Incorporation, and held on   ,   (year), it was

resolved by the vote of the holders of an appropriate majority of the shares of each class

entitled to vote that ARTICLE   of the Articles of Incorporation is amended

to read as follows:

ARTICLE

Signed on

By_____
President

_____
Secretary

CERTIFICATE OF DISSOLUTION

_____

WE, the President and Secretary of   , in accordance
with the requirements of the Corporation Law of the State of   and for
purposes of obtaining the dissolution of said Corporation, as provided by said Law,

DO HEREBY CERTIFY AS FOLLOWS:

The registered office of   in the State of
            is at   .

The agent in charge thereof, upon whom process against this Corporation may be
served, is   ,   ,
      .

The dissolution of said   has been duly authorized
under the provisions of Section   of Corporation Law of the State of
      .

The following are the names and residences of all the directors of the said Corporation:

            NAME   ADDRESS

Dated: _____
                                    President

                                    _____
                                    Secretary

INCUMBENCY CERTIFICATE

I, _____ , Secretary of _____ ,
do hereby affirm and verify that the duly constituted officers of the Corporation as of
_____ , _____ (year), are:

_____ , President

_____ , Vice President

_____ , Treasurer

_____ , Secretary

A True Record:

Attest:

_____
Secretary

State of

County of

On _____ before me, _____ ,
personally appeared

_____ ,

who personally known to me (or proved to me on the basis of satisfactory evidence) to be
the person(s) whose name(s) is/are subscribed to the within instrument and acknowledged
to me that he/she/they executed the same in his/her/their authorized capacity(ies), and
that by his/her/their signature(s) on the instrument the person(s), or the entity upon
behalf of which the person(s) acted, executed the instrument.
WITNESS my hand and official seal.

Signature_____
My commission expires:

Affiant _____Known _____Produced ID
Type of ID _____

(Seal)

NOTICE TO OFFICER OF REMOVAL FROM BOARD

Date:

To:

    PLEASE TAKE NOTICE that, pursuant to Article   , Section   of the Bylaws of this Corporation, the Board of Directors did, at a meeting held on   ,   (year), adopt a resolution removing you forthwith from the office of director, a copy of which resolution is annexed hereto and the original of which is on file in the principal office of the Corporation.

_____

Secretary

RESOLUTION:
ACCEPT DIRECTOR'S RESIGNATION

RESOLVED, that the resignation of _____ as a member of the

Board of Directors of the Corporation as evidenced by a resignation letter to the

Corporation, dated _____ , _____ (year), is hereby accepted, and the

Secretary of the Corporation is hereby instructed to notify _____ of

the Board's acceptance.

The undersigned hereby certifies that he/she is the duly elected and qualified Secretary

and the custodian of the books and records and seal of _____ ,

a corporation duly formed pursuant to the laws of the State of _____ ,

and that the foregoing is a true record of a resolution duly adopted at a meeting of the

Board of Directors, and that said meeting was held in accordance with state law and the

Bylaws of the above-named Corporation on _____ , _____ (year), and that

said resolution is now in full force and effect without modification or rescission.

IN WITNESS WHEREOF, I have executed my name as Secretary and have hereunto

affixed the corporate seal of the above-named Corporation this ____ day of _____ ,

_____ (year).

A True Record.

Attest.

_____
Secretary

RESOLUTION:
ACCEPT OFFICER'S RESIGNATION

RESOLVED, that the resignation of   , as

                    of the Corporation as evidenced by a resignation letter to the

Corporation dated   ,   (year), is hereby accepted, and the Secretary

of the Corporation is hereby instructed to notify   of the

acceptance of said resignation and to further notify such public offices as are necessary.

The undersigned hereby certifies that he/she is the duly elected and qualified Secretary

and the custodian of the books and records and seal of   ,

a corporation duly formed pursuant to the laws of the State of   ,

and that the foregoing is a true record of a resolution duly adopted at a meeting of the

Board of Directors, and that said meeting was held in accordance with state law and the

Bylaws of the above-named Corporation on   ,   (year), and that

said resolution is now in full force and effect without modification or rescission.

IN WITNESS WHEREOF, I have executed my name as Secretary and have hereunto

affixed the corporate seal of the above-named Corporation this   day of   ,

        (year).

A True Record.

Attest.

_____
Secretary

RESOLUTION:
ADOPT AMENDMENT TO ARTICLES

RESOLVED, to amend the Articles of Incorporation in accordance with the proposed amendment as set forth on annexed document, and to duly file necessary notices of amendment with the Division of Corporations.

The undersigned hereby certifies that he/she is the duly elected and qualified Secretary and the custodian of the books and records and seal of   ,

a corporation duly formed pursuant to the laws of the State of   ,

and that the foregoing is a true record of a resolution duly adopted at a meeting of the Board of Directors, and that said meeting was held in accordance with state law and the Bylaws of the above-named Corporation on   ,   (year), and that said resolution is now in full force and effect without modification or rescission.

IN WITNESS WHEREOF, I have executed my name as Secretary and have hereunto affixed the corporate seal of the above-named Corporation this   day of   ,

(year).

A True Record.

Attest.

_____
Secretary

FORM R204

RESOLUTION:
ADOPT SEAL

WHEREAS, this Corporation wishes to adopt a corporate seal as its official mark, be it

RESOLVED, that the following mark constitutes the official seal of the Corporation:

The undersigned hereby certifies that he/she is the duly elected and qualified Secretary

and the custodian of the books and records and seal of   ,

a corporation duly formed pursuant to the laws of the State of   ,

and that the foregoing is a true record of a resolution duly adopted at a meeting of the

Board of Directors, and that said meeting was held in accordance with state law and the

Bylaws of the above-named Corporation on   ,   (year), and that

said resolution is now in full force and effect without modification or rescission.

IN WITNESS WHEREOF, I have executed my name as Secretary and have hereunto

affixed the corporate seal of the above-named Corporation this   day of   ,

(year).

A True Record.

Attest.

_____
Secretary

RESOLUTION:
AMEND ARTICLES OF INCORPORATION

WHEREAS, this Corporation wishes to change its Articles of Incorporation, be it

RESOLVED, to amend the Articles of Incorporation in accordance with the proposed amendment as set forth on annexed document, and to duly file necessary notices of amendment with the Division of Corporations.

The undersigned hereby certifies that he/she is the duly elected and qualified Secretary and the custodian of the books and records and seal of   ,
a corporation duly formed pursuant to the laws of the State of   ,
and that the foregoing is a true record of a resolution duly adopted at a meeting of the Stockholders, and that said meeting was held in accordance with state law and the Bylaws of the above-named Corporation on   ,   (year), and that said resolution is now in full force and effect without modification or rescission.

IN WITNESS WHEREOF, I have executed my name as Secretary and have hereunto affixed the corporate seal of the above-named Corporation this   day of   ,
(year).

A True Record.

Attest.

_____
Secretary

RESOLUTION:
AMEND BYLAWS

WHEREAS, this Corporation wishes to change its Bylaws, be it

RESOLVED, that the Corporation change its Bylaws in accordance with the proposed amendments to Bylaws as annexed hereto, and

FURTHER RESOLVED, that the proper officers of the Corporation file said amended Bylaws with such parties who are, pursuant to law, required to receive or approve same.

The undersigned hereby certifies that he/she is the duly elected and qualified Secretary and the custodian of the books and records and seal of   ,
a corporation duly formed pursuant to the laws of the State of   ,
and that the foregoing is a true record of a resolution duly adopted at a meeting of the Stockholders, and that said meeting was held in accordance with state law and the Bylaws of the above-named Corporation on   ,   (year), and that said resolution is now in full force and effect without modification or rescission.

IN WITNESS WHEREOF, I have executed my name as Secretary and have hereunto affixed the corporate seal of the above-named Corporation this   day of   ,
        (year).

A True Record.

Attest.

_____
                                          Secretary

RESOLUTION:
AMEND BYLAWS WITH SHAREHOLDER APPROVAL

RESOLVED, that, in the judgment of the Board of Directors, it is deemed advisable to amend the Bylaws to provide   , and for that purpose to change Sections   of Article   of the said Bylaws to read as follows:

RESOLVED FURTHER, that a special meeting of the stockholders of this Corporation is hereby called at the office of the Corporation at

            on   ,   (year), at   .m., to take action upon the foregoing resolution, and that the Secretary of the Corporation is hereby directed to give written notice of the said meeting to all stockholders of the Corporation.

The undersigned hereby certifies that he/she is the duly elected and qualified Secretary and the custodian of the books and records and seal of   ,
a corporation duly formed pursuant to the laws of the State of   ,
and that the foregoing is a true record of a resolution duly adopted at a meeting of the Board of Directors, and that said meeting was held in accordance with state law and the Bylaws of the above-named Corporation on   ,   (year), and that said resolution is now in full force and effect without modification or rescission.

IN WITNESS WHEREOF, I have executed my name as Secretary and have hereunto affixed the corporate seal of the above-named Corporation this   day of   ,

        (year).

A True Record.

Attest.

_____
Secretary

RESOLUTION:
AUTHORIZE APPOINTMENT OF DIRECTOR OR OFFICER

Upon motion duly made and seconded, the Board of Directors of

Corporation unanimously adopted the following resolution:

RESOLVED, that   be

appointed the   of

Corporation, and shall hold office until the next annual shareholders' meeting.

shall have the authority to perform the following duties while holding

office:

and such other duties in the management of the corporation as may be required by the

Articles of Incorporation, the Bylaws or by resolution of the Board of Directors of the

corporation.

The undersigned hereby certifies that he/she is the duly elected and qualified Secretary

and the custodian of the books and records and seal of   ,

a corporation duly formed pursuant to the laws of the State of   ,

and that the foregoing is a true record of a resolution duly adopted at a meeting of the

Board of Directors, and that said meeting was held in accordance with state law and the

Bylaws of the above-named Corporation on   ,   , and that said

resolution is now in full force and effect without modification or rescission.

IN WITNESS WHEREOF, I have executed my name as Secretary and have hereunto

affixed the corporate seal of the above-named Corporation this   day of   ,

(year).

A True Record.

Attest.

_____

Secretary

RESOLUTION:
BLANKET AUTHORITY TO AMEND BYLAWS

WHEREAS, the Stockholders of the Corporation understand the Board of Directors may from time to time deem it necessary to change the Bylaws of the Corporation, be it

RESOLVED, that the Board of Directors is hereby authorized and empowered to amend, alter, change, add to, repeal or rescind any and all Bylaws of said corporation from time to time as the Board of Directors deems proper without action or consent on the part of the stockholders, and be it

FURTHER RESOLVED, that the stockholders reserve the right to revoke the above grant of power to the Directors by resolution duly passed at any subsequent stockholder meeting, but until such revocation, the stockholders shall not exercise their power to amend, alter, change, add to, repeal or rescind the Bylaws of the Corporation presently contained in Article _____ of said Bylaws.

The undersigned hereby certifies that he/she is the duly elected and qualified Secretary and the custodian of the books and records and seal of _____ ,
a corporation duly formed pursuant to the laws of the State of _____ ,
and that the foregoing is a true record of a resolution duly adopted at a meeting of the Stockholders, and that said meeting was held in accordance with state law and the Bylaws of the above-named Corporation on _____ , _____ (year), and that said resolution is now in full force and effect without modification or rescission.

IN WITNESS WHEREOF, I have executed my name as Secretary and have hereunto affixed the corporate seal of the above-named Corporation this _____ day of _____ ,

_____ (year).

A True Record.

Attest.

_____
Secretary

RESOLUTION:
CHANGE AMOUNT OF AUTHORIZED SHARES

WHEREAS, this Corporation wishes to change the number of authorized shares, be it

RESOLVED, to change the number of authorized shares of common stock of the

Corporation from   shares to   shares, and to obtain such

authorizations as are necessary from the Division of Corporations and to pay any fees

associated therewith.

The undersigned hereby certifies that he/she is the duly elected and qualified Secretary

and the custodian of the books and records and seal of   ,

a corporation duly formed pursuant to the laws of the State of   ,

and that the foregoing is a true record of a resolution duly adopted at a meeting of the

Stockholders, and that said meeting was held in accordance with state law and the Bylaws

of the above-named Corporation on   ,   (year), and that said

resolution is now in full force and effect without modification or rescission.

IN WITNESS WHEREOF, I have executed my name as Secretary and have hereunto

affixed the corporate seal of the above-named Corporation this   day of   ,

     (year).

A True Record.

Attest.

                          _____
                          Secretary

RESOLUTION:
CHANGE CORPORATE ADDRESS

RESOLVED, that the Corporation change its official address from

to   , and that said change

of address be duly filed with the Department of Corporations and such further parties who

shall be entitled to notice or wherein notice is desirable as in the best interests of the

Corporation.

The undersigned hereby certifies that he/she is the duly elected and qualified Secretary

and the custodian of the books and records and seal of   ,

a corporation duly formed pursuant to the laws of the State of   ,

and that the foregoing is a true record of a resolution duly adopted at a meeting of the

Board of Directors, and that said meeting was held in accordance with state law and the

Bylaws of the above-named Corporation on   ,   (year), and that

said resolution is now in full force and effect without modification or rescission.

IN WITNESS WHEREOF, I have executed my name as Secretary and have hereunto

affixed the corporate seal of the above-named Corporation this   day of   ,

(year).

A True Record.

Attest.

_____
Secretary

RESOLUTION:
CHANGE CORPORATE NAME

RESOLUTION:

That the Corporation change its corporate name from

to _____ ; and that said change of name be

duly filed with the Department of Corporations in accordance with State law and such

other governmental agencies as may be required to be notified of or to approve said name

change.

The undersigned hereby certifies that he/she is the duly elected and qualified Secretary

and the custodian of the books and records and seal of _____ ,

a corporation duly formed pursuant to the laws of the State of _____ ,

and that the foregoing is a true record of a resolution duly adopted at a meeting of the

Board of Directors, and that said meeting was held in accordance with state law and the

Bylaws of the above-named Corporation on _____ , _____ (year), and that

said resolution is now in full force and effect without modification or rescission.

IN WITNESS WHEREOF, I have executed my name as Secretary and have hereunto

affixed the corporate seal of the above-named Corporation this ____ day of _____ ,

____ (year).

A True Record.

Attest.

_____
Secretary

RESOLUTION:
CHANGE FISCAL YEAR

WHEREAS, the Corporation would gain certain accounting and tax benefits from a change in fiscal year; be it

RESOLVED, that the Corporation change its fiscal year from the twelve month period ending _____ of each year to the twelve month period ending _____ of each year, and that said change of fiscal year be recorded with the Department of Corporations.

The undersigned hereby certifies that he/she is the duly elected and qualified Secretary and the custodian of the books and records and seal of _____ , a corporation duly formed pursuant to the laws of the State of _____ , and that the foregoing is a true record of a resolution duly adopted at a meeting of the Board of Directors, and that said meeting was held in accordance with state law and the Bylaws of the above-named Corporation on _____ , _____ (year), and that said resolution is now in full force and effect without modification or rescission.

IN WITNESS WHEREOF, I have executed my name as Secretary and have hereunto affixed the corporate seal of the above-named Corporation this _____ day of _____ , _____ (year).

A True Record.

Attest.

_____
Secretary

RESOLUTION:
CHANGE NUMBER OF AUTHORIZED SHARES

RESOLVED, to change the number of authorized shares of common stock of the

Corporation from   shares to   shares, and to obtain such

authorizations as are necessary from the Division of Corporations and to pay any fees

associated therewith.

The undersigned hereby certifies that he/she is the duly elected and qualified Secretary

and the custodian of the books and records and seal of   ,

a corporation duly formed pursuant to the laws of the State of   ,

and that the foregoing is a true record of a resolution duly adopted at a meeting of the

Board of Directors, and that said meeting was held in accordance with state law and the

Bylaws of the above-named Corporation on   ,   (year), and that

said resolution is now in full force and effect without modification or rescission.

IN WITNESS WHEREOF, I have executed my name as Secretary and have hereunto

affixed the corporate seal of the above-named Corporation this   day of   ,

        (year).

A True Record.

Attest.

_____
Secretary

RESOLUTION:
DISSOLVE CORPORATION WITH SHAREHOLDER APPROVAL

RESOLVED, that in the judgment of the Board of Directors it is deemed advisable that this Corporation should be dissolved; and as required by law, it is ordered that a meeting of those stockholders of said Corporation having voting power to take action upon this resolution is hereby called, to be held at the office of said Corporation at

, on   ,   (year) , at   .m., and

RESOLVED FURTHER, that the Secretary of this Corporation is hereby authorized and directed, within   (   ) days after its adoption, this resolution be mailed to each stockholder of this Corporation, and also within   (   ) days after the adoption of this resolution, to cause notice of the time appointed for said meeting to be inserted in a newspaper published in the County of   ,
State of   , once a week, for at least   (   ) successive weeks preceding the meeting.

The undersigned hereby certifies that he/she is the duly elected and qualified Secretary and the custodian of the books and records and seal of   ,
a corporation duly formed pursuant to the laws of the State of   ,
and that the foregoing is a true record of a resolution duly adopted at a meeting of the Board of Directors, and that said meeting was held in accordance with state law and the Bylaws of the above-named Corporation on   ,   (year), and that said resolution is now in full force and effect without modification or rescission.

IN WITNESS WHEREOF, I have executed my name as Secretary and have hereunto affixed the corporate seal of the above-named Corporation this   day of   ,
        (year).

A True Record.

Attest.

_____
Secretary

RESOLUTION:
EXTEND APPOINTMENT

WHEREAS, _____ has had an appointment to serve the

Corporation as _____ for a _____ year period due to terminate on

_____ , _____ (year) , and

WHEREAS, _____ has requested an extension of said

appointment and an extension would also be to the advantage of the Corporation; be it

RESOLVED, that the Corporation extend the appointment of _____

for a period of _____ , upon such compensation, benefits and terms as

presently in effect.

The undersigned hereby certifies that he/she is the duly elected and qualified Secretary

and the custodian of the books and records and seal of _____ ,

a corporation duly formed pursuant to the laws of the State of _____ ,

and that the foregoing is a true record of a resolution duly adopted at a meeting of the

Board of Directors, and that said meeting was held in accordance with state law and the

Bylaws of the above-named Corporation on _____ , _____ (year), and that

said resolution is now in full force and effect without modification or rescission.

IN WITNESS WHEREOF, I have executed my name as Secretary and have hereunto

affixed the corporate seal of the above-named Corporation this _____ day of _____ ,

_____ (year).

A True Record.

Attest.

_____
Secretary

RESOLUTION:
FILL VACANCY ON BOARD

RESOLVED, that   is hereby appointed a director of the Corporation until the next annual stockholders' meeting, to fill the vacancy caused by the resignation of   .

The undersigned hereby certifies that he/she is the duly elected and qualified Secretary and the custodian of the books and records and seal of   ,
a corporation duly formed pursuant to the laws of the State of   ,
and that the foregoing is a true record of a resolution duly adopted at a meeting of the Board of Directors, and that said meeting was held in accordance with state law and the Bylaws of the above-named Corporation on   ,   (year), and that said resolution is now in full force and effect without modification or rescission.

IN WITNESS WHEREOF, I have executed my name as Secretary and have hereunto affixed the corporate seal of the above-named Corporation this   day of   ,
     (year).

A True Record.

Attest.

_____
Secretary

RESOLUTION:
OBTAIN "S" CORPORATION STATUS

WHEREAS, there would be certain tax and financial benefits to the shareholders of the Corporation upon an election to have the Corporation qualify as an "S" Corporation pursuant to Section 1362 of the Internal Revenue Code; be it

RESOLVED, to qualify the Corporation as an "S" Corporation pursuant to Section 1362 of the Internal Revenue Code.

The undersigned hereby certifies that he/she is the duly elected and qualified Secretary and the custodian of the books and records and seal of   ,
a corporation duly formed pursuant to the laws of the State of   ,
and that the foregoing is a true record of a resolution duly adopted at a meeting of the Stockholders, and that said meeting was held in accordance with state law and the Bylaws of the above-named Corporation on   ,   (year), and that said resolution is now in full force and effect without modification or rescission.

IN WITNESS WHEREOF, I have executed my name as Secretary and have hereunto affixed the corporate seal of the above-named Corporation this   day of   ,
        (year).

A True Record.

Attest.

_____
Secretary

RESOLUTION:
REMOVE AN OFFICER OR DIRECTOR

RESOLVED, that _____ is hereby removed from office as

_____ of this Corporation, effective herewith, and

RESOLVED FURTHER, that the Secretary of this Corporation is hereby directed to give

notice of such removal to the said _____ .

The undersigned hereby certifies that he/she is the duly elected and qualified Secretary

and the custodian of the books and records and seal of _____ ,

a corporation duly formed pursuant to the laws of the State of _____ ,

and that the foregoing is a true record of a resolution duly adopted at a meeting of the

Board of Directors, and that said meeting was held in accordance with state law and the

Bylaws of the above-named Corporation on _____ , _____ (year), and that

said resolution is now in full force and effect without modification or rescission.

IN WITNESS WHEREOF, I have executed my name as Secretary and have hereunto

affixed the corporate seal of the above-named Corporation this _____ day of _____ ,

_____ (year).

A True Record.

Attest.

_____
Secretary

RESOLUTION:
REQUEST RESIGNATION OF OFFICER

RESOLVED, that   is hereby requested to resign as

of the Corporation, effective immediately, and the

Secretary of the Corporation is hereby directed to send a copy of this resolution to the said

.

The undersigned hereby certifies that he/she is the duly elected and qualified Secretary

and the custodian of the books and records and seal of   ,

a corporation duly formed pursuant to the laws of the State of   ,

and that the foregoing is a true record of a resolution duly adopted at a meeting of the

Board of Directors, and that said meeting was held in accordance with state law and the

Bylaws of the above-named Corporation on   ,   (year), and that

said resolution is now in full force and effect without modification or rescission.

IN WITNESS WHEREOF, I have executed my name as Secretary and have hereunto

affixed the corporate seal of the above-named Corporation this   day of   ,

(year).

A True Record.

Attest.

_____
Secretary

RESOLUTION:
TERMINATE FOREIGN CORPORATION STATUS

WHEREAS, the Corporation has or shall discontinue the conduct of business within the

State of _____ ; be it

RESOLVED, to have the Corporation terminate its status as a foreign Corporation in the

State of _____ .

The undersigned hereby certifies that he/she is the duly elected and qualified Secretary

and the custodian of the books and records and seal of _____ ,

a corporation duly formed pursuant to the laws of the State of _____ ,

and that the foregoing is a true record of a resolution duly adopted at a meeting of the

Board of Directors, and that said meeting was held in accordance with state law and the

Bylaws of the above-named Corporation on _____ , _____ (year), and that

said resolution is now in full force and effect without modification or rescission.

IN WITNESS WHEREOF, I have executed my name as Secretary and have hereunto

affixed the corporate seal of the above-named Corporation this _____ day of _____ ,

_____ (year).

A True Record.

Attest.

_____
                                                        Secretary

RESOLUTION:
TERMINATE "S" CORPORATION STATUS

WHEREAS, there are no longer benefits to the shareholders of the Corporation to have the Corporation qualify as an "S" Corporation, and it is desirable to have the Corporation operate as a "C" Corporation; be it

RESOLVED, to terminate the Corporation as an "S" Corporation under Section 1362 of the Internal Revenue Code.

The undersigned hereby certifies that he/she is the duly elected and qualified Secretary and the custodian of the books and records and seal of
, a corporation duly formed pursuant to the laws of the State of
, and that the foregoing is a true record of a resolution duly adopted at a meeting of the Stockholders, and that said meeting was held in accordance with state law and the Bylaws of the above-named Corporation on   ,   (year), and that said resolution is now in full force and effect without modification or rescission.

IN WITNESS WHEREOF, I have executed my name as Secretary and have hereunto affixed the corporate seal of the above-named Corporation this   day of   ,

        (year).

A True Record.

Attest.

_____
                                        Secretary

Minutes
of
meetings

3

Chapter 3

Minutes of meetings

Forms in this chapter:

MINUTES, FIRST MEETING OF DIRECTORS

_____

The first meeting of the Board of Directors of

Corporation was held at   , in the City of   ,

State of   , on the   day of   ,   (year), at

         .m.

There were present: ,   ,

and   , being all of the directors of

Corporation.

Upon motion duly made, seconded and carried,   acted as

temporary chairman, and   acted as temporary secretary of the

meeting.

The Secretary put forth and read a waiver of notice of the meeting, signed by all the

directors.

The minutes of the meeting of incorporators and subscribers to the capital stock were

read and approved.

Upon motion duly made, seconded and carried, it was

RESOLVED, that the acts of the incorporators of

Corporation,   and   , jointly and severally, for and on behalf of the Corporation, are hereby approved, ratified and adopted as acts of the Corporation, in the same manner as if each and every such act has been done pursuant to the specific authorization of the Corporation.

Upon motion duly made, seconded and carried, it was

RESOLVED, that all action taken by the incorporators, stockholders and subscribers to capital stock of the Corporation at the organization meeting held at

on the   day of   ,   (year), be and the same are hereby approved and ratified to the full extent that approval and ratification by this Board of Directors is necessary or proper.

Upon motion duly made, seconded and carried, it was

RESOLVED, that the Treasurer is hereby authorized to pay or reimburse all fees and expenses incident to and necessary for the organization of the Corporation, and to procure and pay for the proper corporate books.

Upon motion duly made, seconded and carried, it was

RESOLVED, that the Bylaws for the regulation and management of the affairs of the Corporation, which were read and approved and adopted article by article be filed with the minutes of this meeting and authenticated as the corporate Bylaws by the signature of the Secretary of this meeting.

Upon motion duly made, seconded and carried, it was

RESOLVED, that an election be held to choose a Chairman of the Board of Directors, a President, an Executive Vice President, a Vice President, a Secretary-Treasurer, to serve for a period of one year and thereafter until their respective successors shall be elected and qualify.

The following persons were nominated officers of the Corporation:

Name   Office

_____   _____

_____   _____

_____   _____

_____   _____

The Chairman announced that the aforementioned persons had been elected to the office set opposite their respective names.

Each of the officers so elected thereupon accepted the office to which elected as aforestated.

_____ moved to consider the salaries of the officers of the Corporation of the year commencing _____, _____ (year). The motion was duly seconded and carried. The Chairman announced that the officer whose salary was being considered would not participate in the vote, and that the salary of each officer would be considered separately.

, President, having left the meeting, it was on motion duly made, seconded and carried:

That the salary of   as President of

Corporation, beginning   ,   (year), and ending   ,

(year), be fixed at   Dollars ($) per

year, payable in installments of   Dollars ($) on the

day of each and every   .

The salary of   as President of

Corporation, having been duly voted upon,   was recalled to the

meeting.

, Vice President of the Corporation then left the meeting.

, Vice President, having left the meeting, it was on motion duly

made, seconded and carried:

That the salary of   as Vice President of

Corporation, beginning   ,   (year), and ending   ,

(year), be fixed at   Dollars ($) per

year, payable in installments of   Dollars ($) on the

day of each and every   .

The salary of   as Vice President of

Corporation, having been duly voted upon,   was recalled to the

meeting.

, Secretary-Treasurer of the Corporation, then left the meeting.

, Secretary-Treasurer, having left the meeting, it was on motion duly made, seconded and carried:

That the salary of _____, Secretary-Treasurer of _____ Corporation, beginning _____, _____ (year), and ending _____, _____ (year), be fixed at _____ Dollars ($ _____) per year, payable in installments of _____ Dollars ($ _____) on the day of each and every _____ .

The salary of _____, Secretary-Treasurer of _____ Corporation, having been duly voted upon, _____ was recalled to the meeting.

On motions duly made and seconded it was resolved

1. That the seal, an impression whereof is hereto attached, be adopted as the corporate seal of this Corporation.

2. A form of stock certificate was presented and adopted.

3. That the stock book and transfer book presented to the Board at this meeting are hereby adopted as the stock book and transfer book of the Corporation.

4. That the Corporation shall act as its own transfer agent, and

5. That the President shall have the power when necessary to employ one or more transfer clerks, or to assign the duties of a transfer clerk to one or more officers or employees of the Corporation, furthermore to discharge the transfer clerk or clerks, or to revoke the duties of transfer clerk granted to any officer or employee.

6. That the Board of Directors is hereby authorized and directed to issue and sell, at a consideration fixed by the Board, however, at no less than the par-value of the stock, the entire unsubscribed and unissued authorized capital

stock of this Corporation, amounting to   shares of Common
Stock with a par value of   Dollar(s) per share; and

7.   That the President and Secretary are directed to take all necessary action to comply with the Securities Laws of the United States and the State of   before issuing or selling any of said stock.

8.   That the Board of Directors is hereby authorized and directed to issue the remainder of the unissued authorized capital stock of this Corporation, from time to time as may be desirable in its discretion, upon payment therefor of a good and fair consideration fixed by the Board.

WHEREAS,   has offered to purchase all the unsubscribed and unissued shares of common stock of Corporation for the price of $ per share, payable in cash,

AND WHEREAS, the Board of Directors of this Corporation deem such a sale desirable:

That the Board of Directors is hereby authorized to accept the offer of   and to issue to said offerer   shares of common stock, and the certificate evidencing the same upon full payment of the agreed price.

9.   That the principal office of the Corporation in   be established and maintained at   , in the City of

10.   That the fiscal year of the Corporation begin on the first day of in each year.

11. That the _____ Bank located at _____ (hereinafter "Bank") is hereby designated as a depository of this Corporation and that the officers and agents of this Corporation are hereby authorized to deposit any and all of the funds of this Corporation in said Bank either at its head office or at any of its branches.

12. That any funds of this Corporation deposited in said Bank be subject to withdrawal or charge at any time and from time to time upon checks, notes, drafts, bills of exchange, acceptances, undertakings, or other instruments or orders for the payment of money when made, signed, drawn, accepted or endorsed on behalf of this Corporation by any two of the following officers: President, Vice President, Secretary-Treasurer.

13. That the Bank is hereby authorized to pay any such instrument or make any such charge and also to receive the same from the payee or any other holder without inquiry as to the circumstances of issue or the disposition of the proceeds even if drawn to the individual order of any signing person, or payable to said Bank or others for his account, or tendered in payment of his individual obligation, and whether drawn against an account in the name of this Corporation or in the name of any officer or agent of this Corporation as such.

14. That any two of the following: the President, Vice President, Secretary-Treasurer are hereby authorized on behalf of this Corporation:

A. To borrow money and to obtain credit for the Corporation from the Bank on any terms and to make and deliver notes, drafts, acceptances, instruments of guaranty, agreements and any other obligations of this Corporation therefore in form satisfactory to the Bank.

B. To pledge or assign and deliver, as security for money borrowed or credit obtained, stocks, bonds, bills receivable, accounts, mortgages, merchandise, bills-of-lading, warehouse receipts, insurance policies, certificates, and any other property held by or belonging to the Corporation with full authority to endorse, assign, or guarantee the same in the name of the Corporation.

C. To discount any bills receivable or any paper held by the Corporation with full authority to endorse the same in the name of the Corporation.

D. To withdraw from the Bank and give receipt for, or to authorize the Bank to deliver to bearer or to one or more designated persons, all or any documents and securities or other property held by it, whether held as collateral security or for safekeeping or for any other purpose.

E. To authorize the Bank to purchase or sell for account of the Corporation stocks, bonds and other securities, and

F. To execute and deliver all instruments required by the Bank in connection with any of the foregoing matters and affix thereto the seal of this Corporation.

15. That the Secretary or any other officer of this Corporation is hereby authorized to certify to the Bank the names of the present officers of this Corporation and other persons authorized to sign for it and the offices respectively held by them, together with specimens of their signatures, and in case of any change of any holder of any such office or holders of any such offices, the fact of such change and the names of any new officers and the offices respectively held by them, together with specimens of their signatures;

and the Bank is hereby authorized to honor any instrument signed by any new officer or officers in respect of whom it has received any such certificate or certificates with the same force and effect as if said officer or said officers were named in the foregoing resolutions in the place of any person or persons with the same title or titles.

16. That the Bank be promptly notified in writing by the Secretary or any officer of this Corporation of any change in these resolutions, such notice to be given to each office of the Bank in which any account of this Corporation may be kept, and that until it has actually received such notice in writing it is authorized to act in pursuance of these resolutions, and that until it has actually so received such notice it shall be indemnified and saved harmless from any loss suffered or liability incurred by it in continuing to act in pursuance of these resolutions, not withstanding, that these resolutions may have been changed.

17. That, beginning with the present meeting, the fees of non-salaried members of the Board of Directors be fixed at $ per meeting.

Upon motion duly made, seconded and carried, it was further resolved

18. That   be engaged to make the annual audit of the books of this Corporation for the year ending   ,   (year), and that   be paid the sum of

Dollars ($) for such services; and that the proper officers of this Corporation are hereby authorized and directed to execute a written retainer for said services of   .

There being no further business, a motion was duly made, seconded and carried that the meeting be adjourned.

_____   _____
President   Secretary

MINUTES OF ANNUAL MEETING OF STOCKHOLDERS

_____

The annual meeting of stockholders of   was held

at   at

        .m., on   ,   (year).

The meeting was called to order by   , President, who

chaired the meeting, and   , Secretary, kept the record of the meeting.

The Secretary stated that the following stockholders were present in person:

Names	Number of Shares
_____	_____
_____	_____
_____	_____
_____	_____

and that the following stockholders were represented by proxy:

Names	Number of Proxies	Number of Shares
_____	_____	_____
_____	_____	_____
_____	_____	_____

The Chairman then reported that there were present in person and represented by proxy the number of shares necessary to constitute a quorum to conduct business.

The proxies presented were directed to be filed with the Secretary of the meeting.

The Chairman then stated that the next business to come before the meeting was the election of the Board of Directors to serve for the upcoming year.

The following were nominated as directors:

_____

_____

_____

No other persons were nominated.

Upon motion duly made, seconded and unanimously carried, the nominations were closed.

The ballots of the stockholders were presented and the Secretary reported that

_____ ,   and   had

received a plurality of the votes.

The Chairman then declared that the aforementioned persons were duly elected directors of the Corporation to hold office for the upcoming year.

No further business coming before the meeting, upon motion duly made, seconded and carried, the meeting adjourned.

_____
Secretary

FORM M303

MINUTES OF COMBINED MEETING
OF
STOCKHOLDERS AND DIRECTORS

A combined meeting of Stockholders and Directors was held at the office of the

Corporation at   on   ,

(year), at   .m.

The following Directors were present at the meeting:

_____   _____

_____   _____

_____   _____

being a quorum of the Directors of the Corporation.

The following Shareholders were present in person or by proxy at the meeting:

_____   _____

_____   _____

_____   _____

being a quorum of the Shareholders of the Corporation.

                              , President of the Corporation, acted as Chairman of the

meeting, and   , Secretary of the Corporation, acted as

Secretary of the meeting.

The Secretary presented notice or waiver of notice of the meeting, signed by all interested parties.

The meeting, having been duly convened, was ready to proceed with its business, whereupon it was resolved:

The Secretary announced that _____ shares of common stock had been voted in favor of the foregoing resolution(s) and _____ shares of common stock had been voted against the resolution(s), said vote representing more than _____ % of the outstanding shares entitled to vote thereon.

The President thereupon declared that the resolution(s) had been duly adopted.

There being no further business, upon motion, the meeting was adjourned.

_____
Secretary

MINUTES OF DIRECTORS' MEETINGS

_____

A regular meeting of the Board of Directors of

was held at   on   ,

(year), at   .m.

The following were present and participating at the meeting:

_____

_____

_____

being all the directors of the Corporation.

, President of the Corporation, acted as Chairman of the

meeting, and   , Secretary of the Corporation, acted as Secretary of the

meeting.

The Secretary put forth a waiver of notice of the meeting, signed by all the directors, and accordingly filed the waiver of notice with the minutes of the meeting.

The Chairman stated that a quorum of the directors was present, and that the meeting, having been duly convened, could transact business.

The minutes of the regular meeting of the directors held on   ,

(year), were read and approved.

WHEREAS, the accumulated surplus of the Corporation is

Dollars ($).

RESOLVED, that a dividend of   cents per share is hereby declared on the outstanding capital stock of this Corporation, that said dividend will be paid on

,   (year), to stockholders of record at the close of business on

,   (year); and

RESOLVED FURTHER, that the Secretary is hereby authorized and instructed to notify said stockholders of the declaration of said dividend, and the Treasurer is hereby authorized and instructed to pay said dividend on said date.

A motion was duly made and carried to consider the salaries of the officers of the Corporation for the year commencing on   ,   (year). The Chairman stated that the officer whose salary was being considered would not participate in the vote, and that the salary of each officer would be considered separately.

, President, having left the meeting, it was on motion duly made, seconded and carried:

That the salary of   , as President of the Corporation, be fixed at   Dollars ($) per year.

The salary of   , as President of the Corporation, having been duly voted upon,   was recalled to the meeting.

, Vice President of the Corporation, then left the meeting.

, Vice President having left the meeting, it was on motion duly made, seconded and carried:

That the salary of   , as Vice President of the Corporation, be fixed at   Dollars ($) per year.

The salary of   , as Vice President of the Corporation, having been duly voted upon,   was recalled to the meeting.

, Treasurer of the Corporation, then left the meeting.

, Treasurer having left the meeting, it was on motion duly made, seconded and carried:

That the salary of   , as Treasurer of the Corporation, be fixed at   Dollars ($) per year.

The salary of   , as Treasurer of the Corporation, having been duly voted upon,   was recalled to the meeting.

, Secretary of the Corporation, then left the meeting.

, Secretary having left the meeting, it was on motion duly made, seconded and carried:

That the salary of   , as Secretary of the Corporation, be fixed at

                                                      Dollars ($)

per year.

The salary of   , as Secretary of the Corporation, having been

duly voted upon,   was recalled to the meeting.

There being no further business, the meeting was adjourned.

_____

Chairman

_____

Secretary

MINUTES OF ORGANIZATION MEETING
OF BOARD OF DIRECTORS

of _____

The organizational meeting of the Board of Directors of

was held at   on   ,

(year), at   .m.

Present were   ,   ,   ,

being the persons designated as the Directors in the Articles of Incorporation.

acted as temporary Chairman of the meeting and

acted as temporary Secretary.

The Chairman stated that the meeting had been duly called by the Incorporators of the Corporation.

The Chairman announced that the Articles of Incorporation of the Corporation had been duly filed with the State of   on   ,

(year)   . The Certificate of Incorporation and a copy of said Articles of Incorporation were directed to be inserted in the Minutes and made a part thereof.

A proposed form of Bylaws for the regulation and the management of the affairs of the Corporation was put forth at the meeting. The Bylaws were read and deliberated and, upon motion duly made and seconded, it was:

RESOLVED, that the form of Bylaws of the Corporation, as put forth in this meeting, a copy of which is ordered to be inserted in the Minute Book of the Corporation, and the same are hereby approved and adopted as the Bylaws of the Corporation.

The following persons were nominated officers of the Corporation to serve until their respective successors are chosen and qualify:

PRESIDENT:

VICE PRESIDENT:

SECRETARY:

TREASURER:

The Chairman announced that said persons had been elected to the office set opposite their respective names.

The President thereupon took the chair and the Secretary immediately assumed the discharge of the duties of that office.

The President then announced that there were a number of organizational matters to be deliberated at the meeting and a number of resolutions to be approved and adopted by the Board of Directors.

The form of stock certificates was then exhibited at the meeting. Thereupon, a motion duly made and seconded, it was:

RESOLVED, that the form of stock certificates put forth at this meeting be, and the same is hereby adopted and approved as the stock certificate of the Corporation, a specimen copy of the stock certificate to be attached with these Minutes.

FURTHER RESOLVED, that the officers are hereby authorized and directed to pay or reimburse the payment of all fees and expenses incident to and necessary for the organization of this Corporation.

The Board of Directors then considered the opening of a corporate bank account to serve as a depository for the funds of the Corporation. Following deliberation, on motion duly made and seconded, it was:

RESOLVED, that the Treasurer be authorized and directed to open an account with and to deposit all funds of the Corporation, all drafts, checks and notes of the Corporation payable on said account to be made in the corporate name signed by   .

FURTHER RESOLVED, that officers are hereby authorized to execute such resolutions (including formal Bank Resolutions), documents and other instruments as may be necessary or advisable in opening or continuing said bank account. A copy of the applicable printed form of Bank Resolution hereby adopted to supplement these Minutes is ordered attached to the Minutes of this meeting.

It is reported that the following persons have made an offer to transfer the property listed below in exchange for the following shares of the stock of the Corporation:

Name	Payment Consideration, or Property	Number of Shares

Upon motion duly made and seconded, it was:

RESOLVED, that acceptance of the offer of the aforementioned persons is in the best interest of the Corporation and necessary for carrying out the corporate business, and in the judgment of the Board of Directors, the assets proposed to be transferred to the Corporation are reasonably worth the amount of consideration deemed therefore, and the same hereby is accepted, and that upon receipt of the consideration indicated above, the President and the Secretary are authorized and directed to issue certificates of fully paid, nonassessable capital stock of this Corporation in the amounts indicated to the aforementioned persons.

To insure the payment of expenses of incorporation and organization for the Corporation, on motion duly made, seconded and unanimously carried, the following resolution was adopted:

RESOLVED, that the President and the Secretary and/or Treasurer of Corporation be and they are hereby authorized and directed to pay the expenses of this Corporation, including attorney's fees for incorporation, and to reimburse the persons who have made disbursement thereof.

After deliberation of the appropriate issues with regard to the tax year and accounting basis, on motion duly made, seconded and unanimously carried, the following resolution was adopted:

RESOLVED, that the first fiscal year of the Corporation shall commence on

            and end on   .

FURTHER RESOLVED, that the President be and is hereby authorized and directed to enter into employment contracts with certain employees, such contract shall be for the term and the rate stated in the attached Employment Agreements.

FURTHER RESOLVED, that it shall be the policy of the Corporation to reimburse each employee or to pay directly on his behalf all expenses incidental to his attendance at conventions and seminars as may be approved by the President. Reimbursement shall include full reimbursement for commercial and private transportation, expenses, plus other necessary and ordinary out-of-pocket expenses incidental to the said travel, including meals and lodging.

A deliberation was then held concerning the immediate commencement of business operations as a Corporation and it was then decided that business operations of the Corporation would commence as of   .

It was agreed that no fixed date would be set for holding meetings of the Board of Directors except the regular meetings to be held immediately after the annual meetings of shareholders as provided in the Bylaws of the Corporation but that meetings of the Directors would be periodically called by the President and Secretary or others pursuant to the Bylaws.

Upon motion duly made, seconded and unanimously carried, it was:

RESOLVED, that the officers of the Corporation are hereby authorized and empowered to do any and all things necessary to conduct the business of the Corporation as set forth in the Articles of Incorporation and Bylaws of the Corporation.

Upon motion duly made, seconded and unanimously carried, the following resolution was adopted:

RESOLVED, that, if required,   be, and hereby is, appointed Resident Agent in the State of   . The office of the Resident Agent will be located at   .

The Chairman then announced at the meeting the question of electing the provisions of Section 1244 of the Internal Revenue Code. He stated that this Section permits ordinary loss treatment when either the holder of Section 1244 stock sells or exchanges such stock at a loss or when such stock becomes worthless. After deliberation, the following preamble was announced and the following resolution was unanimously approved:

RESOLVED, that:

WHEREAS, this Corporation qualifies as a small business corporation as defined in Section 1244, but

WHEREAS, the Board of Directors are concerned over future tax law changes modifying Section 1244 as presently enacted (subsequent to the Revenue Act of 1978) and thus desire to safeguard this Corporation's 1244 election by complying with prior law as well as present law, and

WHEREAS, pursuant to the requirements of Section 1244 and the Regulations issued thereunder, the following plan has been presented to the Corporation by the Board of Directors of the Corporation:

(a)   The plan as hereafter set forth shall, upon its adoption by the Board of Directors of the Corporation, immediately become effective.

(b)   No more than   shares of common stock are authorized to be issued under this plan, and such stock shall have a par value of $ per share.

(c)   Stock authorized under this plan shall be issued only in exchange for money, or property subject to monetary valuation other than capital stock, securities or services rendered or to be rendered. The aggregate dollar amount to be received for such stock shall not exceed $1,000,000, and the sum of each aggregate dollar amount and the equity capital of the Corporation (determined on the date of adoption of the plan) shall not exceed $1,000,000.

(d)   Any stock options granted during the life of this plan which apply to the stock issuable hereunder shall apply solely to such stock and to no other and must be exercised within the period in which the plan is effective.

(e)   Such other action as may be necessary shall be taken by the Corporation to qualify the stock to be offered and issued under this plan as "Section 1244 Stock," as such term is defined in the Internal Revenue Code and the regulations issued thereunder.

NOW, THEREFORE, said plan to issue Section 1244 Stock is adopted by the Corporation and the appropriate officers of the Corporation are authorized and directed to take all actions deemed by them necessary to carry out the intent and purpose of the recited plan.

There being no further business requiring Board action or consideration, the meeting was adjourned.

Dated:

_____
Secretary

MINUTES OF SPECIAL MEETING OF DIRECTORS

_____

A special meeting of the Board of Directors of   was

held at the office of the Corporation,   ,

on   ,   (year), at   .m.

The following directors were present and participating at the meeting:

_____

_____

_____

being all of the directors of the Corporation.

                              , President of the Corporation, acted as Chairman of the

meeting, and   , Secretary of the Corporation, acted as Secretary of the

meeting.

The Secretary put forth and read a waiver of notice of the meeting signed by all the directors, and accordingly, filed a copy of the waiver with the minutes of the meeting.

The Chairman stated that a quorum of the directors was present, and that the meeting, having been duly convened, could transact business.

On the motion duly made and seconded, and after due deliberation, the following resolution was adopted:

There being no further business, the meeting was adjourned.

_____
                                          Secretary

FORM M307

MINUTES OF SPECIAL MEETING OF STOCKHOLDERS

_____

A special meeting of the stockholders was duly called and held at

_____ , in the City of _____ , in the State of _____ ,

on _____ , _____ (year), at _____ .m.

The meeting was called to order by _____ , the President of the

Corporation, and _____ , the Secretary of the Corporation, kept the

records of the meeting and its proceedings.

The Secretary noted that stockholders owning _____ shares were present in

person and stockholders owning _____ shares were represented by proxy, the

aggregate amount representing more than _____ percent of the outstanding stock

entitled to vote on the amendment to the articles of incorporation proposed at the meeting.

The secretary stated that the following stockholders were present in person:

Names	Number of Shares
_____	_____
_____	_____
_____	_____

and that the following stockholders were represented by proxy:

Names	Names of Proxies	Number of Shares
_____	_____	_____
_____	_____	_____
_____	_____	_____

The Chairman then reported that there were present in person and represented by proxy the number of shares necessary to constitute a quorum to conduct business.

The Secretary put forth and read a waiver of notice of the meeting signed by each stockholder entitled to notice of the meeting, said waiver of notice together with a copy of the proxies submitted at the meeting were directed to be filed with the minutes of the meeting.

On the motion duly made and seconded, and after due deliberation, the following resolution was made:

A vote was taken which showed:

In Favor of Motion

_____, representing   shares

_____, representing   shares

_____, representing   shares

Opposed to Motion

_____, representing   shares

_____, representing   shares

Not Voting on Motion

_____, representing   shares

The Secretary announced that   shares of common stock had been voted in favor of the said resolution and   shares of common stock had been voted against said resolution, said vote representing more than   percent of outstanding shares in attendance and entitled to vote thereon.

The President thereafter declared that the resolution had been duly adopted.

There being no further business, upon motion duly made, the meeting adjourned.

_____
Secretary

NOTICE OF ANNUAL SHAREHOLDERS' MEETING

Notice is hereby given that the annual meeting of shareholders of

shall be held on   ,   (year), at   .m.,

in the offices of the Corporation at   ,

in the City of   .

The shareholders will deliberate and take action on the following matters:

    1.   The election of a new Board of Directors for the year beginning   ,

           (year), and ending   ,   (year).

    2.   Transact such other business as may properly come before the meeting or any

           adjournment thereof.

Only those shareholders who were shareholders of record at the close of business on

          ,   (year), will be entitled to vote in person or by proxy at the

meeting or any adjournment thereof.

               By order of the Board of Directors

               of   Corporation

               _____

               Secretary

Dated:

NOTICE OF MEETING—DIRECTORS

A meeting of the Board of Directors of   , will be held

on   ,   (year), at   .m., in the offices of the

Corporation located at   for the

following matter:

Dated:

_____
Secretary

NOTICE OF ORGANIZATION MEETING
OF INCORPORATORS AND DIRECTORS

TO: _____

_____

_____

You are hereby notified that:

We, the undersigned, do hereby constitute a majority of the directors named in the Articles of Incorporation of _____, a corporation.

Pursuant to state law, we are hereby calling an organization meeting of the Board of Directors and incorporators named in the Articles of Incorporation of the above-named corporation. The purpose of said meeting is to adopt Bylaws, elect officers, and transact such other business as may come before the meeting; and

Said organization meeting shall be held at _____ _____ on _____, _____ (year), at _____ .m.

_____   _____

_____   _____

RECEIPT OF NOTICE

_____   _____

Address-Director   Date Received

FORM N304

NOTICE OF WAIVER OF
ANNUAL MEETING BY ALL SHAREHOLDERS

We, the undersigned, being the holders of all of the outstanding shares of stock of

_____ , do hereby waive notice of the annual meeting of shareholders

scheduled to be held in the office of the Corporation at _____ ,

in the City of _____ , on _____ , _____ (year), at _____ .m.

The undersigned understand that the purposes of the meeting are to:

    (1)   Elect a new board of directors.

    (2)   Conduct any other business that properly may be brought before the
           meeting.

Shareholder	Date	Number of Shares
_____	_____	_____
_____	_____	_____
_____	_____	_____

NOTICE TO DIRECTORS OF SPECIAL MEETING

Date:

A special meeting of the Board of Directors of   will be

held on   ,   (year), at   .m., in the offices of the

Corporation located at   , in the City of

                , to deliberate the following matter:

_____

Secretary

NOTICE TO SHAREHOLDERS OF SPECIAL MEETING

Date:

To the shareholders of   :

A special meeting of the shareholders of   will be

held on   ,   (year), at   .m. in the offices of the

Corporation located at   .

Shareholders will be asked to deliberate and vote upon the following resolution

adopted by the Board of Directors:

The Board of Directors

of   Corporation

_____

Secretary

Only those shareholders who were shareholders of record at the close of business on

the   day of   ,   (year), will be allowed to vote in person or by

proxy at the meeting or any adjournment thereof.

RESOLUTION:
CALL SHAREHOLDERS' MEETING

RESOLVED, that the annual meeting of shareholders of the corporation shall be held on

_____ , _____ (year), at _____ .m. The meeting shall be held at the

offices of the Corporation located at _____ ,

in the City of _____ , _____ .

The purpose of the meeting shall be:

(1) To elect a new board of directors.
(2) Transact such other business that may properly come before the meeting or any adjournment thereof.

Only shareholders who are shareholders of record on the _____ day of _____ ,

19 _____ , shall be entitled to vote at the meeting or any adjournment of the meeting.

The undersigned hereby certifies that he/she is the duly elected and qualified Secretary

and the custodian of the books and records and seal of _____ ,

a corporation duly formed pursuant to the laws of the State of _____ ,

and that the foregoing is a true record of a resolution duly adopted at a meeting of the

Board of Directors, and that said meeting was held in accordance with state law and the

Bylaws of the above-named Corporation on _____ , _____ (year), and that

said resolution is now in full force and effect without modification or rescission.

IN WITNESS WHEREOF, I have executed my name as Secretary and have hereunto

affixed the corporate seal of the above-named Corporation this _____ day of _____ ,

_____ (year).

A True Record.

Attest.

_____
Secretary

RESOLUTION:
CHANGE DATE OF ANNUAL MEETING

WHEREAS, this Corporation wishes to change the date of the annual meeting, be it

RESOLVED, to change the date for the annual meeting of shareholders from   ,

(year), to   ,   (year); and that notice of said change of meeting

date be duly filed with the Division of Corporations, as required by the laws of the State of

.

The undersigned hereby certifies that he/she is the duly elected and qualified Secretary

and the custodian of the books and records and seal of   ,

a corporation duly formed pursuant to the laws of the State of   ,

and that the foregoing is a true record of a resolution duly adopted at a meeting of the

Stockholders, and that said meeting was held in accordance with state law and the Bylaws

of the above-named Corporation on   ,   (year), and that said

resolution is now in full force and effect without modification or rescission.

IN WITNESS WHEREOF, I have executed my name as Secretary and have hereunto

affixed the corporate seal of the above-named Corporation this   day of   ,

(year).

A True Record.

Attest.

_____
                                    Secretary

RESOLUTION:
FIX DATE FOR SHAREHOLDERS ELIGIBLE TO VOTE

WHEREAS, this corporation wishes to fix the date for shareholders to be eligible to vote, be it

RESOLVED, that the close of business on _____ , _____ (year), is hereby fixed as the time and date for determining shareholders who will be entitled to notice of and to the right to vote at at meeting of shareholders that will be held on the day of _____ , _____ (year), in the City of _____ .

The undersigned hereby certifies that he/she is the duly elected and qualified Secretary and the custodian of the books and records and seal of _____ , a corporation duly formed pursuant to the laws of the State of _____ , and that the foregoing is a true record of a resolution duly adopted at a meeting of the Board of Directors, and that said meeting was held in accordance with state law and the Bylaws of the above-named Corporation on _____ , _____ (year), and that said resolution is now in full force and effect without modification or rescission.

IN WITNESS WHEREOF, I have executed my name as Secretary and have hereunto affixed the corporate seal of the above-named Corporation this _____ day of _____ , _____ (year).

A True Record.

Attest.

_____
Secretary

RESOLUTION:
SPECIAL MEETING TO ELECT DIRECTORS

WHEREAS, a board of directors was not elected at the last annual meeting of

shareholders, it is therefore

RESOLVED, that a special meeting of the shareholders of

Corporation shall be held on the   day of   ,   (year), at   .m.,

at the offices of the Corporation,   , in the

City of   , State of   ,

for the sole purpose of electing directors of the corporation.

The undersigned hereby certifies that he/she is the duly elected and qualified Secretary

and the custodian of the books and records and seal of   ,

a corporation duly formed pursuant to the laws of the State of   ,

and that the foregoing is a true record of a resolution duly adopted at a meeting of the

Board of Directors, and that said meeting was held in accordance with state law and the

Bylaws of the above-named Corporation on   ,   (year), and that

said resolution is now in full force and effect without modification or rescision.

IN WITNESS WHEREOF, I have executed my name as Secretary and have hereunto

affixed the corporate seal of the above-named Corporation this   day of   ,

     (year).

A True Record.

Attest.

_____

Secretary

RESOLUTION:
SPECIAL SHAREHOLDERS' MEETING

WHEREAS, the Board of Directors has adopted the following resolution:

RESOLVED, that a special meeting of the shareholders of the Corporation shall be held to deliberate said resolution. The special meeting shall be held at the offices of the Corporation, which are located at   , in the City of   , on   ,   (year), at   .m.

The undersigned hereby certifies that he/she is the duly elected and qualified Secretary and the custodian of the books and records and seal of   , a corporation duly formed pursuant to the laws of the State of   and that the foregoing is a true record of a resolution duly adopted at a meeting of the Board of Directors, and that said meeting was held in accordance with state law and the Bylaws of the above-named Corporation on   ,   (year), and that said resolution is now in full force and effect without modification or rescission.

IN WITNESS WHEREOF, I have executed my name as Secretary and have hereunto affixed the corporate seal of the above-named Corporation this   day of   ,   (year).

A True Record.

Attest.

_____
Secretary

WAIVER OF NOTICE — COMBINED MEETING

I, the undersigned, the holder of   shares of stock of

and/or a Board of Director, do hereby waive notice of the combined meeting of

shareholders and board of directors of the said corporation.

Furthermore, the undersigned hereby agrees that said meeting shall be held at   .m.

on   ,   (year), at the following location:

Date: _____   _____

                                         Shareholder/Director

WAIVER OF NOTICE OF ANNUAL MEETING
BY INDIVIDUAL SHAREHOLDER

I, the undersigned, the holder of   shares of stock of

    , do hereby waive notice of the annual meeting of shareholders of the

Corporation which will be held for the following purposes:

(1) Electing a new board of directors.

(2) Transacting any other business that may properly be brought before the meeting.

The undersigned hereby consents to the holding of the meeting on   ,

(year), at   .m. in the offices of the Corporation which are located at

     , in the City of   .

Date: _____

                              Shareholder

WAIVER OF NOTICE OF DIRECTORS' MEETING

The undersigned, constituting the entire membership of the Board of Directors of

_____, hereby waive notice of the meeting of the Board

of Directors of the Corporation and consent to the holding of the meeting at _____ .m.,

on _____, _____ (year), at the offices of the Corporation located at

_____. Furthermore, we agree that

any lawful business may be transacted at the meeting.

Dated:

_____

_____

_____

WAIVER OF NOTICE OF ORGANIZATION
MEETING OF INCORPORATORS AND DIRECTORS

of _____

We do hereby constitute the Incorporators and Directors of the above captioned Corporation and do hereby waive notice of the organization meeting of Directors and Incorporators of the said Corporation.

Furthermore, we hereby agree that said meeting shall be held at _____ .m. on _____ , _____ (year), at the following location: _____

_____ .

We do hereby affix our names to show our waiver of notice of said meeting.

_____   _____
Incorporator   Director

_____   _____
Incorporator   Director

Dated:

WRITTEN UNANIMOUS CONSENT IN LIEU OF MEETING

The undersigned, being the holders of all of the outstanding shares of

_____ Corporation entitled to vote at a meeting of shareholders, do hereby

consent to the following resolution adopted by the Board of Directors of

_____ Corporation taken on _____ , _____ (year):

Signed:_____

_____

_____

Dated: _____ , _____ (year)

Stockholder forms

Chapter 4
Stockholder forms

Forms in this chapter:

DEMAND FOR INSPECTION OF
CORPORATE BOOKS AND RECORDS

The undersigned, _____ , is the holder of _____ shares of

the common stock of _____ and does hereby demand the

opportunity to inspect, at the office of the Corporation, the books and records of the

Corporation, its stock ledger and the list of its shareholders. The undersigned does further

state that the inspection is sought for a proper purpose, to wit:

The undersigned also states that he has never sold nor offered for sale any list of

shareholders of any corporation, nor assisted any person in obtaining such a list or record

for such purposes.

The requested date and time for inspection is:

   Date: _____

   Time: _____

State of
County of

   On _____ before me, _____

, who personally known to me (or proved to me on the basis of satisfactory evidence) to
be the person(s) whose name(s) is/are subscribed to the within instrument and
acknowledged to me that he/she/they executed the same in his/her/their authorized
capacity(ies), and that by his/her/their signature(s) on the instrument the person(s), or the
entity upon behalf of which the person(s) acted, executed the instrument.
WITNESS my hand and official seal.

Signature_____

My commission expires: _____   Affiant _____Known _____Produced ID
                                            Type of ID _____
                                                                    (Seal)

IRREVOCABLE PROXY

I, _____ , the holder of _____ shares of the common voting stock of _____ Corporation, do hereby irrevocably appoint _____ as my proxy to attend the shareholders' meeting of _____ Corporation, to be held on _____ , _____ (year), or any continuations or adjournments of that meeting, with full power to vote and act for me and in my name and place, in the same manner, and to the same extent that I might act if I would have been in attendance at such meeting.

This proxy is irrevocable and has been issued to _____ who is a pledgee holding a valid pledge of the shares owned by me. Any other proxy or proxies previously given by me to others is hereby revoked.

Dated:

_____

State of
County of

On _____ before me,
_____ , personally appeared

_____ , who personally known to me (or proved to me on the basis of satisfactory evidence) to be the person(s) whose name(s) is/are subscribed to the within instrument and acknowledged to me that he/she/they executed the same in his/her/their authorized capacity(ies), and that by his/her/their signature(s) on the instrument the person(s), or the entity upon behalf of which the person(s) acted, executed the instrument.
WITNESS my hand and official seal.
Signature_____
My commission expires: _____ Affiant _____Known
_____Produced ID

Type of ID _____

(Seal)

LIST OF SHAREHOLDERS

I, _____ , Secretary of

_____ Corporation, hereby certify the following list of shareholders who own all outstanding

stock of the Corporation and who are entitled to vote at the shareholders' meeting on the

_____ day of _____ , _____ (year), because they were shareholders of record

at the close of business on the _____ day of _____ , _____ (year).

Shareholder	Total Number of Shares Owned	Total Number of Voting Shares Owned
_____	_____	_____
_____	_____	_____
_____	_____	_____
_____	_____	_____

Dated: _____

_____
Secretary of the Corporation

PROXY TO VOTE SHARES

The undersigned, as owner of   shares of common voting stock in

(Corporation), represented by Share Certificate No.

, hereby authorizes   to vote those shares at the meeting of

shareholders of the said Corporation to be held on the   day of

,   (year), at   .m., or any adjournment thereto, at

in the City of   . Under this authority,

shall have the right to vote for the election of directors and on any other matter as may

properly be raised at the meeting, all with the same force and effect as if I were voting said

shares personally.

_____

State of

County of

   On   before me,   ,
personally appeared   ,
who personally known to me (or proved to me on the basis of satisfactory evidence) to be
the person(s) whose name(s) is/are subscribed to the within instrument and acknowledged
to me that he/she/they executed the same in his/her/their authorized capacity(ies), and
that by his/her/their signature(s) on the instrument the person(s), or the entity upon
behalf of which the person(s) acted, executed the instrument.
WITNESS my hand and official seal.

Signature_____

My commission expires: Affiant _____Known _____Produced ID
                                            Type of ID _____

REVOCATION OF PROXY

I, _____, the holder of _____ shares of common voting stock of _____ (Corporation), having appointed _____ to act as my proxy by a written proxy dated _____, _____ (year), a copy of which is attached, do hereby revoke that proxy.

IN WITNESS WHEREOF, I do hereby execute this revocation of proxy in duplicate on this, the _____ day of _____, _____ (year). The original of this revocation shall be filed in the office of _____ Corporation, and the duplicate copy of this revocation shall be delivered by Certified Return Receipt mail, to _____, the person named by me as my proxy in the revoked proxy agreement.

_____

State of
County of

On _____ before me, _____,
personally appeared _____,
who personally known to me (or proved to me on the basis of satisfactory evidence) to be the person(s) whose name(s) is/are subscribed to the within instrument and acknowledged to me that he/she/they executed the same in his/her/their authorized capacity(ies), and that by his/her/their signature(s) on the instrument the person(s), or the entity upon behalf of which the person(s) acted, executed the instrument.
WITNESS my hand and official seal.

Signature_____
My commission expires: _____

Affiant _____ Known _____ Produced ID
Type of ID _____

(Seal)

STOCK SUBSCRIPTION

I,_____, the undersigned do hereby subscribe for

the purchase of   (   ) shares of the common stock of

_____(Corporation) at $_____ per share, for the aggregate purchase

price of $. I understand that upon issue, said shares shall constitute   %

of the common shares outstanding and entitled to vote and that there are no other shares

outstanding.

_____
Subscriber

The foregoing subscription is accepted and the Treasurer shall issue said shares upon

payment to the corporation the sum of $.

_____
For the Corporation
and its Board of Directors

Operations

Chapter 5
Operations

Forms in this chapter:

RESOLUTION:
ACQUIRE ASSETS OF BUSINESS

WHEREAS, it is considered advisable for the Corporation to purchase and acquire all or substantially all of the business assets of

, as a going business concern; be it

RESOLVED, that the Corporation execute an agreement to purchase the business assets of   , all in accordance with a purchase agreement annexed hereto; and be it

RESOLVED FURTHER, that the President of the Corporation be authorized to execute such further documents and undertake such other acts as are reasonably required to carry out and consummate said transaction to purchase assets.

RESOLVED, that the Board of Directors be and is authorized and empowered to take all actions necessary to sell and dispose of the assets and properties of the Corporation, all upon such price and terms as the Board in its discretion deems to be in the best interests of the Corporation.

The undersigned hereby certifies that he/she is the duly elected and qualified Secretary and the custodian of the books and records and seal of   ,

a corporation duly formed pursuant to the laws of the State of   ,

and that the foregoing is a true record of a resolution duly adopted at a meeting of the Stockholders, and that said meeting was held in accordance with state law and the Bylaws of the above-named Corporation on   ,   (year), and that said resolution is now in full force and effect without modification or rescission.

IN WITNESS WHEREOF, I have executed my name as Secretary and have hereunto affixed the corporate seal of the above-named Corporation this   day of   ,

        (year).

A True Record.

Attest.

_____
Secretary

RESOLUTION:
ACQUIRE SHARES OF STOCK

WHEREAS, the Board of Directors has determined that it is in the best interests of the Corporation to acquire certain shares of the common stock of

; be it

RESOLVED, that the Corporation acquire   (   ) shares of the common stock of   ; said shares representing

% of all shares, in all classes, outstanding, all for the aggregate purchase price of   Dollars ($) per share, all as more particularly set forth in a stock purchase agreement as annexed hereto; and, be it

RESOLVED FURTHER, that the President and/or Treasurer of the Corporation undertake all actions necessary to carry out said resolution.

The undersigned hereby certifies that he/she is the duly elected and qualified Secretary and the custodian of the books and records and seal of   ,

a corporation duly formed pursuant to the laws of the State of   ,

and that the foregoing is a true record of a resolution duly adopted at a meeting of the Board of Directors, and that said meeting was held in accordance with state law and the Bylaws of the above-named Corporation on   ,   (year), and that said resolution is now in full force and effect without modification or rescission.

IN WITNESS WHEREOF, I have executed my name as Secretary and have hereunto affixed the corporate seal of the above-named Corporation this   day of   ,

     (year).

A True Record.

Attest.

_____
Secretary

RESOLUTION:
ADOPT TRADE NAME

WHEREAS, it is desirous for the Corporation to adopt a trade name and style under which to conduct business; be it

RESOLVED, that the Corporation adopt the trade name:
as an assumed name for the conduct of certain business activities; and, be it

RESOLVED FURTHER, that the President of the Corporation record adoption and use of said fictitious name with the appropriate public records.

The undersigned hereby certifies that he/she is the duly elected and qualified Secretary and the custodian of the books and records and seal of   ,
a corporation duly formed pursuant to the laws of the State of   ,
and that the foregoing is a true record of a resolution duly adopted at a meeting of the Board of Directors, and that said meeting was held in accordance with state law and the Bylaws of the above-named Corporation on   ,   (year), and that said resolution is now in full force and effect without modification or rescission.

IN WITNESS WHEREOF, I have executed my name as Secretary and have hereunto affixed the corporate seal of the above-named Corporation this   day of   ,
(year).

A True Record.

Attest.

_____
Secretary

RESOLUTION:
APPOINT A PURCHASING AGENT

WHEREAS, this Corporation wishes to appoint someone to be in charge of purchases for the Corporation, be it

RESOLVED, that _____ is hereby appointed Purchasing Agent of this Corporation with authority to make purchases in the Corporation's name and behalf. Under no circumstances is the Purchasing Agent to have authority to make a purchase for the Corporation if the dollar amount of the purchase or the total dollar amount of a purchase made in installments will exceed _____ dollars ($ _____).

The undersigned hereby certifies that he/she is the duly elected and qualified Secretary and the custodian of the books and records and seal of _____ , a corporation duly formed pursuant to the laws of the State of _____ , and that the foregoing is a true record of a resolution duly adopted at a meeting of the Board of Directors, and that said meeting was held in accordance with state law and the Bylaws of the above-named Corporation on _____ , _____ (year), and that said resolution is now in full force and effect without modification or rescision.

IN WITNESS WHEREOF, I have executed my name as Secretary and have hereunto affixed the corporate seal of the above-named Corporation this _____ day of _____ ,
(year).

A True Record.

Attest.

_____
Secretary

RESOLUTION:
APPROVE CHAPTER 11 REORGANIZATION PLAN

WHEREAS, the Corporation has formulated a plan of reorganization that it believes is fair and feasible, and

WHEREAS, creditors of the Corporation have indicated support for said plans; be it

RESOLVED, that the Corporation affirms and approves the plan of reorganization under Chapter 11 of the Bankruptcy Code, all as set forth in the terms annexed hereto.

The undersigned hereby certifies that he/she is the duly elected and qualified Secretary and the custodian of the books and records and seal of   , a corporation duly formed pursuant to the laws of the State of   , and that the foregoing is a true record of a resolution duly adopted at a meeting of the Stockholders, and that said meeting was held in accordance with state law and the Bylaws of the above-named Corporation on   ,   (year), and that said resolution is now in full force and effect without modification or rescission.

IN WITNESS WHEREOF, I have executed my name as Secretary and have hereunto affixed the corporate seal of the above-named Corporation this   day of   ,

    (year).

A True Record.

Attest.

_____
Secretary

RESOLUTION:
ASSIGN LEASE

WHEREAS, the Corporation presently holds a lease for space that is no longer required for the conduct of the business; be it

RESOLVED, that the Corporation assign its lease for premises at

to   ; said lease assignment to be

effective   ,   (year), and shall further be upon such terms and conditions as are contained in a certain assignment of lease agreement annexed hereto.

The undersigned hereby certifies that he/she is the duly elected and qualified Secretary and the custodian of the books and records and seal of   ,

a corporation duly formed pursuant to the laws of the State of   ,

and that the foregoing is a true record of a resolution duly adopted at a meeting of the Board of Directors, and that said meeting was held in accordance with state law and the Bylaws of the above-named Corporation on   ,   (year), and that said resolution is now in full force and effect without modification or rescission.

IN WITNESS WHEREOF, I have executed my name as Secretary and have hereunto affixed the corporate seal of the above-named Corporation this   day of   ,

          (year).

A True Record.

Attest

_____
Secretary

RESOLUTION:
AUTHORIZE BORROWING ON LINE OF CREDIT

WHEREAS, this Company desires to borrow money, be it

RESOLVED, that the proper officers of this Company are hereby authorized to borrow

from the   Bank, for and in behalf of this Company, a sum

not to exceed   Dollars ($),

on its promissory note maturing   (   ) days from the date hereof, to

be signed by the proper officers of this Company, and to bear interest not to exceed the rate

of   percent (%) per annum, and with the additional privilege

of renewing the balance of said loan at its maturity, for another period of

(   ) days, and the proper officers of this Company are hereby authorized and

directed to sign any new or renewal note or notes required by said

Bank to carry out the provisions of this resolution, which new note or notes shall bear such

rate of interest as shall be agreed upon between this Company and the

Bank at the time of such renewal or renewals.

The undersigned hereby certifies that he/she is the duly elected and qualified Secretary

and the custodian of the books and records and seal of   ,

a corporation duly formed pursuant to the laws of the State of   ,

and that the foregoing is a true record of a resolution duly adopted at a meeting of the

Board of Directors, and that said meeting was held in accordance with state law and the

Bylaws of the above-named Corporation on   ,   (year), and that

said resolution is now in full force and effect without modification or rescission.

IN WITNESS WHEREOF, I have executed my name as Secretary and have hereunto

affixed the corporate seal of the above-named Corporation this   day of   ,

         (year).

A True Record.

Attest.

_____
Secretary

RESOLUTION:
AUTHORIZE CONTRACT

RESOLVED, that the Corporation enter into a contract with

for the general purposes of:

and all upon

such terms and conditions as are set forth in an agreement between the parties as annexed

hereto.

The undersigned hereby certifies that he/she is the duly elected and qualified Secretary

and the custodian of the books and records and seal of   ,

a corporation duly formed pursuant to the laws of the State of   ,

and that the foregoing is a true record of a resolution duly adopted at a meeting of the

Board of Directors, and that said meeting was held in accordance with state law and the

Bylaws of the above-named Corporation on   ,   (year), and that

said resolution is now in full force and effect without modification or rescission.

IN WITNESS WHEREOF, I have executed my name as Secretary and have hereunto

affixed the corporate seal of the above-named Corporation this   day of   ,

(year).

A True Record.

Attest.

_____

Secretary

RESOLUTION:
AUTHORIZE FRANCHISE AGREEMENT

WHEREAS, the Corporation has the opportunity to become licensed as a franchisee of:

, and

WHEREAS, the Board of Directors of the Corporation has concluded that it would be in the best interest of the Corporation to operate as a licensed franchisee; be it

RESOLVED, that the Corporation enter into a franchise agreement with

, in accordance with the terms and conditions of a franchise agreement presented to and reviewed by the Board and as it is annexed hereto; and, be it

RESOLVED FURTHER, that the President of the Corporation undertake all actions as are necessary to perform the obligations of the Corporation under said agreement.

The undersigned hereby certifies that he/she is the duly elected and qualified Secretary and the custodian of the books and records and seal of   ,

a corporation duly formed pursuant to the laws of the State of   ,

and that the foregoing is a true record of a resolution duly adopted at a meeting of the Stockholders, and that said meeting was held in accordance with state law and the Bylaws of the above-named Corporation on   ,   (year), and that said resolution is now in full force and effect without modification or rescission.

IN WITNESS WHEREOF, I have executed my name as Secretary and have hereunto affixed the corporate seal of the above-named Corporation this   day of   ,

(year).

A True Record.

Attest.

_____
Secretary

RESOLUTION:
AUTHORIZE REPAYMENT PLAN

WHEREAS, the Corporation is in arrears on certain obligations due creditors, and

WHEREAS, the Corporation is desirous of entering into a Repayment Plan with its creditors; be it

RESOLVED, that the Corporation hereby assents to a proposed composition agreement and plan of repayment with its creditors, all as contained in the draft agreement annexed hereto.

The undersigned hereby certifies that he/she is the duly elected and qualified Secretary and the custodian of the books and records and seal of   , a corporation duly formed pursuant to the laws of the State of   , and that the foregoing is a true record of a resolution duly adopted at a meeting of the Board of Directors, and that said meeting was held in accordance with state law and the Bylaws of the above-named Corporation on   ,   (year), and that said resolution is now in full force and effect without modification or rescission.

IN WITNESS WHEREOF, I have executed my name as Secretary and have hereunto affixed the corporate seal of the above-named Corporation this   day of   ,

        (year).

A True Record.

Attest.

_____
Secretary

RESOLUTION:
AUTHORIZE SALE/LEASEBACK

WHEREAS, it is advisable for the Corporation to raise capital through a sale/leaseback of certain of its assets; be it

RESOLVED, that the Corporation sell the following property:

to

for the price of $, and that concurrently the Corporation execute a lease

for said property for a period of   years at a net annual rental not to exceed   %

of the sales price, all in accord with generally prevailing sales/leaseback terms.

The undersigned hereby certifies that he/she is the duly elected and qualified Secretary

and the custodian of the books and records and seal of   ,

a corporation duly formed pursuant to the laws of the State of   ,

and that the foregoing is a true record of a resolution duly adopted at a meeting of the

Board of Directors, and that said meeting was held in accordance with state law and the

Bylaws of the above-named Corporation on   ,   (year), and that

said resolution is now in full force and effect without modification or rescission.

IN WITNESS WHEREOF, I have executed my name as Secretary and have hereunto

affixed the corporate seal of the above-named Corporation this   day of   ,

        (year).

A True Record.

Attest.

_____

Secretary

FORM R512

RESOLUTION:
AUTHORIZE TRUST MORTGAGE

WHEREAS, the Corporation is in arrears on certain obligations due creditors, and

WHEREAS, the Corporation is desirous of entering into a repayment plan with its creditors, and securing said repayment obligation with a security interest on assets of the Corporation; be it

RESOLVED, that the Corporation grant to its assenting creditors a Trust Mortgage in accordance with the terms as set forth in the Trust Mortgage annexed hereto.

The undersigned hereby certifies that he/she is the duly elected and qualified Secretary and the custodian of the books and records and seal of   ,
a corporation duly formed pursuant to the laws of the State of   ,
and that the foregoing is a true record of a resolution duly adopted at a meeting of the Board of Directors, and that said meeting was held in accordance with state law and the Bylaws of the above-named Corporation on   ,   (year), and that said resolution is now in full force and effect without modification or rescission.

IN WITNESS WHEREOF, I have executed my name as Secretary and have hereunto affixed the corporate seal of the above-named Corporation this   day of   ,
(year).

A True Record.

Attest.

_____
Secretary

RESOLUTION:
BLANKET AUTHORITY TO SELL ASSETS

RESOLVED, that the Board of Directors is hereby authorized to sell all or any part of the property and assets of this Corporation, including its good will, upon such terms and conditions and for such consideration as the Board of Directors shall deem in the best interests of the Corporation, and more especially, but without limitation of the foregoing, to sell its assets to:

The undersigned hereby certifies that he/she is the duly elected and qualified Secretary and the custodian of the books and records and seal of _____ ,
a corporation duly formed pursuant to the laws of the State of _____ ,
and that the foregoing is a true record of a resolution duly adopted at a meeting of the Stockholders, and that said meeting was held in accordance with state law and the Bylaws of the above-named Corporation on _____ , _____ (year), and that said resolution is now in full force and effect without modification or rescission.

IN WITNESS WHEREOF, I have executed my name as Secretary and have hereunto affixed the corporate seal of the above-named Corporation this ____ day of _____ , ____ (year).

A True Record.

Attest.

_____
Secretary

RESOLUTION:
BORROW AGAINST ACCOUNTS RECEIVABLE

WHEREAS, the Corporation is or may be in need of additional operating funds; be it

RESOLVED, that the Corporation, through   , is hereby authorized to borrow, from time to time, such sums as may be advisable or necessary for the proper operation of the business, said borrowing to be upon such terms and conditions as   may deem appropriate, and for that purpose the Corporation may assign and pledge its accounts receivable as collateral security.

The undersigned hereby certifies that he/she is the duly elected and qualified Secretary and the custodian of the books and records and seal of   , a corporation duly formed pursuant to the laws of the State of   , and that the foregoing is a true record of a resolution duly adopted at a meeting of the Stockholders, and that said meeting was held in accordance with state law and the Bylaws of the above-named Corporation on   ,   (year), and that said resolution is now in full force and effect without modification or rescission.

IN WITNESS WHEREOF, I have executed my name as Secretary and have hereunto affixed the corporate seal of the above-named Corporation this   day of   , (year).

A True Record.

Attest.

_____
Secretary

RESOLUTION:
BORROW CAPITAL

WHEREAS, the Corporation is in need of additional capital, and

WHEREAS,   , as   of the Corporation, has agreed to loan to the Corporation the sum of $, and

WHEREAS, such borrowing appears to be advantageous to the Corporation as it is on better terms than would be available elsewhere; be it

RESOLVED, that the Corporation borrow the sum of $ from   , and that said sum be repaid in or within   years with interest thereon at   % on the unpaid balance, all as more fully set forth in a promissory note and collateral loan documents as have been presented to and reviewed by this Board.

The undersigned hereby certifies that he/she is the duly elected and qualified Secretary and the custodian of the books and records and seal of   , a corporation duly formed pursuant to the laws of the State of   , and that the foregoing is a true record of a resolution duly adopted at a meeting of the Board of Directors, and that said meeting was held in accordance with state law and the Bylaws of the above-named Corporation on   ,   (year), and that said resolution is now in full force and effect without modification or rescission.

IN WITNESS WHEREOF, I have executed my name as Secretary and have hereunto affixed the corporate seal of the above-named Corporation this   day of   , (year).

A True Record.

Attest.

_____
Secretary

RESOLUTION:
BORROW FROM DESIGNATED BANK

RESOLVED, that the   of the Corporation is authorized, for the account of this Corporation, and on such terms and conditions as he/she may deem proper, to borrow from   (Bank) sums of money; and to sign, execute, and endorse all such documents as may be required by said bank to evidence such indebtedness; to discount or rediscount with said bank any of the bills receivable owned by this Corporation; to apply for and obtain from said bank letters of credit, and to execute agreements to secure said bank in connection therewith; to pledge and/or mortgage any moneys on deposit or any moneys otherwise in the possession of said band, and/or any bonds, stocks, receivables, or other property of this Corporation, to secure the payment of any indebtedness, liability, or obligation of this Corporation to said bank whether now due or to become due and whether existing or hereafter incurred, to withdraw and/or substitute any property held at any time by said bank as collateral, and to sign and execute trust receipts for the withdrawal of same when required; and generally to do and perform all acts and sign all agreements, obligations, pledges, and/or other instruments necessary or required by said bank.

The undersigned hereby certifies that he/she is the duly elected and qualified Secretary and the custodian of the books and records and seal of   , a corporation duly formed pursuant to the laws of the State of   , and that the foregoing is a true record of a resolution duly adopted at a meeting of the Board of Directors, and that said meeting was held in accordance with state law and the Bylaws of the above-named Corporation on   ,   (year), and that said resolution is now in full force and effect without modification or rescission.

IN WITNESS WHEREOF, I have executed my name as Secretary and have hereunto affixed the corporate seal of the above-named Corporation this   day of   , (year).

A True Record.

Attest.

_____
Secretary

RESOLUTION:
BORROW ON INVENTORY AND EQUIPMENT

WHEREAS, this Corporation wishes to borrow for corporate purposes, be it

RESOLVED, that   , the President of this

Corporation, is hereby authorized and directed to borrow the sum of

Dollars ($) from

on the terms set out in the Promissory Note attached to the minutes of this meeting and to

execute a mortgage in favor of the Lender covering the furniture, fixtures and inventory of

merchandise set out in the Schedule attached to the minutes of this meeting, and it is

FURTHER RESOLVED, that the President of the Corporation is hereby authorized and

directed to provide for creditors of the Corporation all notices required by law to be given

to the creditors of the Corporation, and to do everything else that may be necessary to

complete the authorized transaction.

The undersigned hereby certifies that he/she is the duly elected and qualified Secretary

and the custodian of the books and records and seal of   ,

a corporation duly formed pursuant to the laws of the State of   ,

and that the foregoing is a true record of a resolution duly adopted at a meeting of the

Stockholders, and that said meeting was held in accordance with state law and the Bylaws

of the above-named Corporation on   ,   (year), and that said

resolution is now in full force and effect without modification or rescission.

IN WITNESS WHEREOF, I have executed my name as Secretary and have hereunto

affixed the corporate seal of the above-named Corporation this   day of   ,

(year).

A True Record.

Attest.

_____
Secretary

RESOLUTION:
COMMENCE LITIGATION

WHEREAS, based on advice of counsel, the Corporation believes it has a valid claim

against   summarily arising from

                                             , be it

RESOLVED, that the Corporation pursue its claim, through court proceedings, if

necessary; and that it be

FURTHER RESOLVED, that   act as counsel for the

Corporation on said matter upon such fee arrangement as may be customarily prevailing

and agreeable to the President of the Corporation; and that it be

FURTHER RESOLVED, that the President of the Corporation, upon the

recommendation of counsel, be authorized to settle said claim for such amount and on

such terms as the President deems to be in the best interests of the Corporation.

The undersigned hereby certifies that he/she is the duly elected and qualified Secretary

and the custodian of the books and records and seal of   ,

a corporation duly formed pursuant to the laws of the State of   ,

and that the foregoing is a true record of a resolution duly adopted at a meeting of the

Board of Directors, and that said meeting was held in accordance with state law and the

Bylaws of the above-named Corporation on   ,   (year), and that

said resolution is now in full force and effect without modification or rescission.

IN WITNESS WHEREOF, I have executed my name as Secretary and have hereunto

affixed the corporate seal of the above-named Corporation this   day of   ,

          (year).

A True Record.

Attest.

_____
Secretary

RESOLUTION:
CONVERT EXCESS DEPRECIATION TO SURPLUS

WHEREAS   dollars ($)

has been assigned to the depreciation account on the Corporation's books for the period

running from   ,   (year), to   ,   (year),

and

WHEREAS   dollars ($)

has been assigned to the reserve for depreciation on the books of the Corporation, and

WHEREAS the value of the real property upon which said depreciation and reserve for

depreciation charges and credits were made has been determined to be

              dollars ($), it is hereby

RESOLVED that the Treasurer of this Corporation is hereby authorized and directed to

transfer on the Corporation's books

dollars ($) from the Corporation's reserve for buildings account to the

Corporation's surplus account.

The undersigned hereby certifies that he/she is the duly elected and qualified Secretary

and the custodian of the books and records and seal of   ,

a corporation duly formed pursuant to the laws of the State of   ,

and that the foregoing is a true record of a resolution duly adopted at a meeting of the

Board of Directors, and that said meeting was held in accordance with state law and the

Bylaws of the above-named Corporation on   ,   (year), and that

said resolution is now in full force and effect without modification or rescission.

IN WITNESS WHEREOF, I have executed my name as Secretary and have hereunto

affixed the corporate seal of the above-named Corporation this   day of   ,

(year).

A True Record.

Attest.

_____
Secretary

RESOLUTION:
DEFEND SUIT

WHEREAS, a claim has been made by   against the

Corporation, which claim summarily asserts:

                                                                          , and

WHEREAS, it is believed that the Corporation has a valid and good defense against

said claim; it is

RESOLVED, that the Corporation defend against said claim; and it is

RESOLVED, that the Corporation retain   as attorneys to

defend said action; and

RESOLVED FURTHER, that the President, upon the recommendation of counsel, be

authorized to compromise and settle said claim for an amount and on such terms as

deemed to be in the best interests of the Corporation.

The undersigned hereby certifies that he/she is the duly elected and qualified Secretary

and the custodian of the books and records and seal of   ,

a corporation duly formed pursuant to the laws of the State of   ,

and that the foregoing is a true record of a resolution duly adopted at a meeting of the

Board of Directors, and that said meeting was held in accordance with state law and the

Bylaws of the above-named Corporation on   ,   (year), and that

said resolution is now in full force and effect without modification or rescission.

IN WITNESS WHEREOF, I have executed my name as Secretary and have hereunto

affixed the corporate seal of the above-named Corporation this   day of   ,

(year).

A True Record.

Attest.

_____
Secretary

RESOLUTION:
EMPLOY

WHEREAS, the Corporation is in need of a   , and

WHEREAS,   has applied for said position and appears well qualified to perform the duties required of said position; be it

RESOLVED, that the Corporation offer   a contract of employment to serve in the capacity of   , at a salary not to exceed $ per year, together with the customary benefits appertaining thereto.

The undersigned hereby certifies that he/she is the duly elected and qualified Secretary and the custodian of the books and records and seal of   , a corporation duly formed pursuant to the laws of the State of   and that the foregoing is a true record of a resolution duly adopted at a meeting of the Board of Directors, and that said meeting was held in accordance with state law and the Bylaws of the above-named Corporation on   ,   (year), and that said resolution is now in full force and effect without modification or rescission.

IN WITNESS WHEREOF, I have executed my name as Secretary and have hereunto affixed the corporate seal of the above-named Corporation this   day of   ,   (year).

A True Record.

Attest.

_____
Secretary

RESOLUTION:
EXERCISE OPTION TO EXTEND LEASE

WHEREAS, the Corporation presently holds a lease due to expire, and

WHEREAS, it is in the best interests of the Corporation to exercise its option to extend the lease; be it

RESOLVED, that the Corporation exercise its option to extend a lease which it holds as tenant from   , as landlord, said lease dated
            ,   (year), for premises at

                                                          .

The undersigned hereby certifies that he/she is the duly elected and qualified Secretary and the custodian of the books and records and seal of   ,
a corporation duly formed pursuant to the laws of the State of   ,
and that the foregoing is a true record of a resolution duly adopted at a meeting of the Board of Directors, and that said meeting was held in accordance with state law and the Bylaws of the above-named Corporation on   ,   (year), and that said resolution is now in full force and effect without modification or rescission.

IN WITNESS WHEREOF, I have executed my name as Secretary and have hereunto affixed the corporate seal of the above-named Corporation this   day of   ,
(year).

A True Record.

Attest.

_____
Secretary

RESOLUTION:
FACTOR ACCOUNTS RECEIVABLE

WHEREAS, it is advisable for the Corporation to raise capital, and

WHEREAS, it is in the best interests of the Corporation to raise said capital through factoring of its accounts receivable; be it

RESOLVED, to factor and assign from time to time all or any part of the accounts receivable of the Corporation to   , pursuant to the terms of a factoring agreement as annexed hereto.

The undersigned hereby certifies that he/she is the duly elected and qualified Secretary and the custodian of the books and records and seal of   ,
a corporation duly formed pursuant to the laws of the State of   ,
and that the foregoing is a true record of a resolution duly adopted at a meeting of the Board of Directors, and that said meeting was held in accordance with state law and the Bylaws of the above-named Corporation on   ,   (year), and that said resolution is now in full force and effect without modification or rescission.

IN WITNESS WHEREOF, I have executed my name as Secretary and have hereunto affixed the corporate seal of the above-named Corporation this   day of   , (year).

A True Record.

Attest.

_____
Secretary

RESOLUTION:
FILE CHAPTER 11 REORGANIZATION

WHEREAS, the Corporation is insolvent and unable to pay its debts when due, and

WHEREAS, the Corporation and its creditors would best be served by reorganization of the Corporation under Chapter 11 of the Bankruptcy Code; be it

RESOLVED, that the Corporation file as soon as practicable for reorganization pursuant to Chapter 11 of the Bankruptcy Code.

The undersigned hereby certifies that he/she is the duly elected and qualified Secretary and the custodian of the books and records and seal of   , a corporation duly formed pursuant to the laws of the State of   , and that the foregoing is a true record of a resolution duly adopted at a meeting of the Stockholders, and that said meeting was held in accordance with state law and the Bylaws of the above-named Corporation on   ,   (year), and that said resolution is now in full force and effect without modification or rescission.

IN WITNESS WHEREOF, I have executed my name as Secretary and have hereunto affixed the corporate seal of the above-named Corporation this   day of   , (year).

A True Record.

Attest.

_____
Secretary

RESOLUTION:
FILE CHAPTER 7 BANKRUPTCY

WHEREAS, the Corporation is insolvent and unable to pay its debts as they mature, and

WHEREAS, it would be in the best interests of creditors for the Corporation to file a voluntary petition under Chapter 7 of the Bankruptcy Code; it is

RESOLVED, that the Corporation file as soon as practicable a bankruptcy in accordance with Chapter 7 of the Bankruptcy Code.

The undersigned hereby certifies that he/she is the duly elected and qualified Secretary and the custodian of the books and records and seal of   ,
a corporation duly formed pursuant to the laws of the State of   ,
and that the foregoing is a true record of a resolution duly adopted at a meeting of the Stockholders, and that said meeting was held in accordance with state law and the Bylaws of the above-named Corporation on   ,   (year), and that said resolution is now in full force and effect without modification or rescission.

IN WITNESS WHEREOF, I have executed my name as Secretary and have hereunto affixed the corporate seal of the above-named Corporation this   day of   ,
        (year).

A True Record.

Attest.

_____
Secretary

RESOLUTION:
FILE FOR RECEIVERSHIP

WHEREAS, the Corporation is insolvent and unable to pay its debts as they become due, and

WHEREAS, it would be in the best interests of creditors to liquidate the assets of the business pursuant to receivership; be it

RESOLVED, that the Corporation file as soon as practicable a petition for receivership in accordance with state laws.

The undersigned hereby certifies that he/she is the duly elected and qualified Secretary and the custodian of the books and records and seal of   ,
a corporation duly formed pursuant to the laws of the State of   ,
and that the foregoing is a true record of a resolution duly adopted at a meeting of the Stockholders, and that said meeting was held in accordance with state law and the Bylaws of the above-named Corporation on   ,   (year), and that said resolution is now in full force and effect without modification or rescission.

IN WITNESS WHEREOF, I have executed my name as Secretary and have hereunto affixed the corporate seal of the above-named Corporation this   day of   ,
(year).

A True Record.

Attest.

_____
Secretary

RESOLUTION:
GRANT MORTGAGE/SECURITY INTEREST

WHEREAS, the Board of Directors has deemed it in the best interests of the Corporation to undertake certain obligations generally referred to:

, and

WHEREAS, it is required that the Corporation pledge certain collateral as security for said obligation; be it

RESOLVED, that the Corporation grant a mortgage or security interest on assets of the Corporation listed and described as:

, and

RESOLVED FURTHER, that the President and/or Treasurer execute and deliver all mortgages, security agreements, loan documents and such related agreements as they deem necessary to secure said obligation as is provided for herein.

The undersigned hereby certifies that he/she is the duly elected and qualified Secretary and the custodian of the books and records and seal of   ,
a corporation duly formed pursuant to the laws of the State of   ,
and that the foregoing is a true record of a resolution duly adopted at a meeting of the Stockholders, and that said meeting was held in accordance with state law and the Bylaws of the above-named Corporation on   ,   (year), and that said resolution is now in full force and effect without modification or rescission.

IN WITNESS WHEREOF, I have executed my name as Secretary and have hereunto affixed the corporate seal of the above-named Corporation this   day of   ,
          (year).

A True Record.

Attest.

_____
Secretary

RESOLUTION:
INDEMNIFY AND SAVE HARMLESS

RESOLVED, that the Corporation indemnify and save harmless

and his or her successors and assigns from any and all liability

arising from:

Said indemnification being upon such terms as are contained in an indemnification

agreement annexed hereto.

The undersigned hereby certifies that he/she is the duly elected and qualified Secretary

and the custodian of the books and records and seal of   ,

a corporation duly formed pursuant to the laws of the State of   ,

and that the foregoing is a true record of a resolution duly adopted at a meeting of the

Board of Directors, and that said meeting was held in accordance with state law and the

Bylaws of the above-named Corporation on   ,   (year), and that

said resolution is now in full force and effect without modification or rescission.

IN WITNESS WHEREOF, I have executed my name as Secretary and have hereunto

affixed the corporate seal of the above-named Corporation this   day of   ,

(year).

A True Record.

Attest.

_____
Secretary

RESOLUTION:
ISSUE GUARANTEE

WHEREAS,   is or shall be indebted to

on an obligation described as: ,

and

WHEREAS, it has been requested that the Corporation issue its guaranty to the

performance of   under said obligation, and

WHEREAS, it is in the best interest of the Corporation to extend its guaranty as

aforesaid; be it

RESOLVED, that the Corporation guarantee the performance of

under said above obligation and that the Corporation execute and deliver the

guaranty as annexed hereto.

The undersigned hereby certifies that he/she is the duly elected and qualified Secretary

and the custodian of the books and records and seal of   ,

a corporation duly formed pursuant to the laws of the State of   ,

and that the foregoing is a true record of a resolution duly adopted at a meeting of the

Board of Directors, and that said meeting was held in accordance with state law and the

Bylaws of the above-named Corporation on   ,   (year), and that

said resolution is now in full force and effect without modification or rescission.

IN WITNESS WHEREOF, I have executed my name as Secretary and have hereunto

affixed the corporate seal of the above-named Corporation this   day of   ,

(year).

A True Record.

Attest.

_____
Secretary

RESOLUTION:
ISSUE OPTION TO BUY SHARES

WHEREAS, in the judgment of the Board of Directors, it is in the best interests of the Corporation to grant to   an option to purchase a certain number of shares of common stock of the Corporation; be it

RESOLVED, that for the good consideration, the Corporation grant and issue to   an option to purchase an aggregate of (   ) shares of the unissued common stock of the Corporation for the option price of $ per share. This option shall terminate on   ,   (year).

The undersigned hereby certifies that he/she is the duly elected and qualified Secretary and the custodian of the books and records and seal of   , a corporation duly formed pursuant to the laws of the State of   , and that the foregoing is a true record of a resolution duly adopted at a meeting of the Stockholders, and that said meeting was held in accordance with state law and the Bylaws of the above-named Corporation on   ,   (year), and that said resolution is now in full force and effect without modification or rescission.

IN WITNESS WHEREOF, I have executed my name as Secretary and have hereunto affixed the corporate seal of the above-named Corporation this   day of   ,   (year).

A True Record.

Attest.

_____
Secretary

RESOLUTION:
ISSUE RELEASE

WHEREAS, a claim has or may arise between the Corporation and

, arising from:

; be it

RESOLVED, that to terminate any possibility of future claim by or against the

Corporation arising from the above, that the Corporation execute and deliver a general

release to the said   , provided the Corporation and its

agents, employees, successors and assigns are simultaneously released by a release signed

by   .

The undersigned hereby certifies that he/she is the duly elected and qualified Secretary

and the custodian of the books and records and seal of   ,

a corporation duly formed pursuant to the laws of the State of   ,

and that the foregoing is a true record of a resolution duly adopted at a meeting of the

Board of Directors, and that said meeting was held in accordance with state law and the

Bylaws of the above-named Corporation on   ,   (year), and that

said resolution is now in full force and effect without modification or rescission.

IN WITNESS WHEREOF, I have executed my name as Secretary and have hereunto

affixed the corporate seal of the above-named Corporation this   day of   ,

(year).

A True Record.

Attest.

_____
Secretary

RESOLUTION:
LEASE AS LESSOR

WHEREAS, the Corporation has available certain space for rental; be it

RESOLVED, that the Corporation, as lessor, lease certain space known as

to

, as lessee; said lease being upon the terms and conditions of a certain lease as annexed

hereto.

The undersigned hereby certifies that he/she is the duly elected and qualified Secretary

and the custodian of the books and records and seal of   ,

a corporation duly formed pursuant to the laws of the State of   ,

and that the foregoing is a true record of a resolution duly adopted at a meeting of the

Board of Directors, and that said meeting was held in accordance with state law and the

Bylaws of the above-named Corporation on   ,   (year), and that

said resolution is now in full force and effect without modification or rescission.

IN WITNESS WHEREOF, I have executed my name as Secretary and have hereunto

affixed the corporate seal of the above-named Corporation this   day of   ,

       (year).

A True Record.

Attest.

_____
Secretary

RESOLUTION:
LEASE EQUIPMENT

WHEREAS, it is necessary to the efficient operation of the business to obtain certain additional equipment; and

WHEREAS, it is more advantageous to the Corporation to lease rather than buy; be it

RESOLVED, to lease certain equipment generally described as

from   , all in accordance with the terms of a certain lease agreement annexed hereto.

The undersigned hereby certifies that he/she is the duly elected and qualified Secretary and the custodian of the books and records and seal of   ,

a corporation duly formed pursuant to the laws of the State of   ,

and that the foregoing is a true record of a resolution duly adopted at a meeting of the Board of Directors, and that said meeting was held in accordance with state law and the Bylaws of the above-named Corporation on   ,   (year), and that said resolution is now in full force and effect without modification or rescission.

IN WITNESS WHEREOF, I have executed my name as Secretary and have hereunto affixed the corporate seal of the above-named Corporation this   day of   ,

(year).

A True Record.

Attest.

_____
Secretary

FORM R534

RESOLUTION:
LEASE MOTOR VEHICLES

WHEREAS, the Corporation has need for an additional motor vehicle, and

WHEREAS, it is more advantageous to the Corporation to lease rather than buy said vehicle; be it

RESOLVED, to lease a motor vehicle described as

, from   , pursuant to the terms of a lease

agreement as annexed hereto.

The undersigned hereby certifies that he/she is the duly elected and qualified Secretary

and the custodian of the books and records and seal of   ,

a corporation duly formed pursuant to the laws of the State of   ,

and that the foregoing is a true record of a resolution duly adopted at a meeting of the

Board of Directors, and that said meeting was held in accordance with state law and the

Bylaws of the above-named Corporation on   ,   (year), and that

said resolution is now in full force and effect without modification or rescission.

IN WITNESS WHEREOF, I have executed my name as Secretary and have hereunto

affixed the corporate seal of the above-named Corporation this   day of   ,

    (year).

A True Record.

Attest.

_____
Secretary

RESOLUTION:
LEASE PREMISES

WHEREAS, the Corporation has certain space requirements as is necessary for the efficient operation of the business; be it

RESOLVED, that the Corporation accept as tenant, a lease from

, as landlord, the premises known as

, in accordance with the terms and conditions of a certain lease as annexed.

The undersigned hereby certifies that he/she is the duly elected and qualified Secretary and the custodian of the books and records and seal of   ,

a corporation duly formed pursuant to the laws of the State of   ,

and that the foregoing is a true record of a resolution duly adopted at a meeting of the Board of Directors, and that said meeting was held in accordance with state law and the Bylaws of the above-named Corporation on   ,   (year), and that said resolution is now in full force and effect without modification or rescission.

IN WITNESS WHEREOF, I have executed my name as Secretary and have hereunto affixed the corporate seal of the above-named Corporation this   day of   ,

(year).

A True Record.

Attest.

_____
Secretary

FORM R536

RESOLUTION:
LOAN FUNDS

WHEREAS, _____ , a _____ of this

Corporation, has requested of this Corporation an advance and loan in the amount of

$ _____ together with interest, and

WHEREAS, the Corporation has adequate financial resources to make such loan

without impairing its growth or profitability, and that said loan is deemed reasonably

secure and in the best interests of the Corporation to make; be it

RESOLVED, that the Corporation issue a loan to _____ , in the amount

of $ _____ , to be repaid within _____ months with interest of ____ % on the unpaid

balance, and that the borrower execute to the Corporation promissory notes evidencing

said indebtedness.

The undersigned hereby certifies that he/she is the duly elected and qualified Secretary

and the custodian of the books and records and seal of _____ ,

a corporation duly formed pursuant to the laws of the State of _____ ,

and that the foregoing is a true record of a resolution duly adopted at a meeting of the

Board of Directors, and that said meeting was held in accordance with state law and the

Bylaws of the above-named Corporation on _____ , _____ (year), and that

said resolution is now in full force and effect without modification or rescission.

IN WITNESS WHEREOF, I have executed my name as Secretary and have hereunto

affixed the corporate seal of the above-named Corporation this ____ day of _____ ,

_____ (year).

A True Record.

Attest.

_____
Secretary

RESOLUTION:
MAKE ASSIGNMENT FOR BENEFIT OF CREDITORS

WHEREAS, the Corporation is insolvent and indebted to numerous creditors, and

WHEREAS, it is in the best interests of creditors as well as the Corporation to liquidate the assets of the Corporation through an assignment for the benefit of creditors; be it

RESOLVED, that the Corporation make a general assignment for the benefit of creditors, naming   as assignee.

The undersigned hereby certifies that he/she is the duly elected and qualified Secretary and the custodian of the books and records and seal of   ,
a corporation duly formed pursuant to the laws of the State of   ,
and that the foregoing is a true record of a resolution duly adopted at a meeting of the Board of Directors, and that said meeting was held in accordance with state law and the Bylaws of the above-named Corporation on   ,   (year), and that said resolution is now in full force and effect without modification or rescission.

IN WITNESS WHEREOF, I have executed my name as Secretary and have hereunto affixed the corporate seal of the above-named Corporation this   day of   ,
        (year).

A True Record.

Attest.

_____
Secretary

RESOLUTION:
MORTGAGE REAL ESTATE

RESOLVED, that the Corporation grant to   a

mortgage on certain real estate known or described as

, and that said mortgage shall be collateral security for a

certain obligation as contained in the documents annexed hereto.

The undersigned hereby certifies that he/she is the duly elected and qualified Secretary

and the custodian of the books and records and seal of   ,

a corporation duly formed pursuant to the laws of the State of   ,

and that the foregoing is a true record of a resolution duly adopted at a meeting of the

Board of Directors, and that said meeting was held in accordance with state law and the

Bylaws of the above-named Corporation on   ,   (year), and that

said resolution is now in full force and effect without modification or rescission.

IN WITNESS WHEREOF, I have executed my name as Secretary and have hereunto

affixed the corporate seal of the above-named Corporation this   day of   ,

    (year).

A True Record.

Attest.

_____
Secretary

RESOLUTION:
NEGOTIATE CONTRACT

RESOLVED, that the President of this Corporation be hereby authorized and empowered to enter into a contract for

with   ,

in the name and in behalf of this Corporation, upon such terms and conditions as may be agreed upon, at the sole discretion of said officer.

The undersigned hereby certifies that he/she is the duly elected and qualified Secretary and the custodian of the books and records and seal of   ,

a corporation duly formed pursuant to the laws of the State of   ,

and that the foregoing is a true record of a resolution duly adopted at a meeting of the Board of Directors, and that said meeting was held in accordance with state law and the Bylaws of the above-named Corporation on   ,   (year), and that said resolution is now in full force and effect without modification or rescission.

IN WITNESS WHEREOF, I have executed my name as Secretary and have hereunto affixed the corporate seal of the above-named Corporation this   day of   ,

(year).

A True Record.

Attest.

_____
Secretary

FORM R540

RESOLUTION:
OBTAIN CORPORATE CHARGE CARD

WHEREAS, it is advisable to obtain charge card privileges for purposes of charging certain expenses relative to the business affairs of the Corporation; be it

RESOLVED, that _____ , as President of the Corporation, apply for and obtain a Corporate Charge Card from _____ with such credit limit as the president deems advisable, and that

NAME   TITLE

_____   _____

_____   _____

_____   _____

be authorized to charge on that account any travel, entertainment and other expenses that are reasonably related to carrying out the business of the Corporation as provided for by the Internal Revenue Code, and that the Treasurer of the Corporation is directed to monitor said account and pay such proper charges as they fall due.

The undersigned hereby certifies that he/she is the duly elected and qualified Secretary and the custodian of the books and records and seal of _____ ,

a corporation duly formed pursuant to the laws of the State of _____ ,

and that the foregoing is a true record of a resolution duly adopted at a meeting of the

Board of Directors, and that said meeting was held in accordance with state law and the

Bylaws of the above-named Corporation on _____, _____ (year), and that

said resolution is now in full force and effect without modification or rescission.

IN WITNESS WHEREOF, I have executed my name as Secretary and have hereunto

affixed the corporate seal of the above-named Corporation this _____ day of _____,

(year).

A True Record.

Attest.

_____
                                                              Secretary

RESOLUTION:
OBTAIN LICENSE

WHEREAS, the Corporation requires certain licenses and permits for the lawful conduct of the activity generally described as:

; be it

RESOLVED, that the Corporation apply to the appropriate governmental agency for such requisite licenses and permits which shall include but not necessarily be limited to:

The undersigned hereby certifies that he/she is the duly elected and qualified Secretary and the custodian of the books and records and seal of   ,
a corporation duly formed pursuant to the laws of the State of   ,
and that the foregoing is a true record of a resolution duly adopted at a meeting of the Board of Directors, and that said meeting was held in accordance with state law and the Bylaws of the above-named Corporation on   ,   (year), and that said resolution is now in full force and effect without modification or rescission.

IN WITNESS WHEREOF, I have executed my name as Secretary and have hereunto affixed the corporate seal of the above-named Corporation this   day of   ,
(year).

A True Record.

Attest.

_____
Secretary

RESOLUTION:
OBTAIN TRADEMARK/SERVICEMARK

WHEREAS, the Corporation has adopted the name

as our identifying mark for the product/service

, and

WHEREAS, the Corporation desires to secure the exclusive rights to said name and/or

mark; be it

RESOLVED, that the Corporation apply to the United States Patent Office for a

trademark/servicemark on:

and that the Corporation undertake all action necessary to successfully obtain and enforce

its trademark application.

The undersigned hereby certifies that he/she is the duly elected and qualified Secretary

and the custodian of the books and records and seal of   ,

a corporation duly formed pursuant to the laws of the State of   ,

and that the foregoing is a true record of a resolution duly adopted at a meeting of the

Board of Directors, and that said meeting was held in accordance with state law and the

Bylaws of the above-named Corporation on   ,   (year), and that

said resolution is now in full force and effect without modification or rescission.

IN WITNESS WHEREOF, I have executed my name as Secretary and have hereunto

affixed the corporate seal of the above-named Corporation this   day of   ,

(year).

A True Record.

Attest.

_____

Secretary

FORM R543

RESOLUTION:
OPEN BANK/CHECKING ACCOUNTS

WHEREAS, the Board of Directors has determined it to be in the best interest of the Corporation to establish a banking resolution with

bank; be it

RESOLVED, that the Corporation execute and deliver to said bank a duly signed original of the completed banking resolution as is annexed hereto, and that the authority to transact business — including but not limited to the maintenance of savings, checking and other accounts as well as borrowing by the Corporation — shall be as contained in said resolution with the named officers therein authorized to so act on behalf of the Corporation as specified thereto.

The undersigned hereby certifies that he/she is the duly elected and qualified Secretary and the custodian of the books and records and seal of   ,

a corporation duly formed pursuant to the laws of the State of   ,

and that the foregoing is a true record of a resolution duly adopted at a meeting of the Stockholders, and that said meeting was held in accordance with state law and the Bylaws of the above-named Corporation on   ,   (year), and that said resolution is now in full force and effect without modification or rescission.

IN WITNESS WHEREOF, I have executed my name as Secretary and have hereunto affixed the corporate seal of the above-named Corporation this   day of   ,

     (year).

A True Record.

Attest.

_____
Secretary

RESOLUTION:
PURCHASE BOAT

WHEREAS, the Board of Directors has determined it to be in the best interests of the Corporation to purchase a boat for purposes of entertaining customers and prospective customers of the Corporation; be it

RESOLVED, that the Corporation purchase a boat on the following specifications:

Year:

Make:

Model:

Length:

Price:

; and, be it

RESOLVED FURTHER, that the President and/or Treasurer of the Corporation maintain accurate records to document use of the boat for legitimate business purposes, and they are further authorized to pay all incidental costs of dockage, storage, insurance, maintenance and repair as is reasonably required to safekeep the value of said boat.

The undersigned hereby certifies that he/she is the duly elected and qualified Secretary and the custodian of the books and records and seal of   ,
a corporation duly formed pursuant to the laws of the State of   ,

and that the foregoing is a true record of a resolution duly adopted at a meeting of the Stockholders, and that said meeting was held in accordance with state law and the Bylaws of the above-named Corporation on   ,   (year), and that said resolution is now in full force and effect without modification or rescission.

IN WITNESS WHEREOF, I have executed my name as Secretary and have hereunto affixed the corporate seal of the above-named Corporation this   day of   ,   (year).

A True Record.

Attest.

_____
Secretary

RESOLUTION:
PURCHASE EQUIPMENT

WHEREAS, it is necessary to purchase certain additional equipment for the efficient

operation of the business; be it

RESOLVED, to purchase certain equipment described generally as

from   for the purchase price

of $.

The undersigned hereby certifies that he/she is the duly elected and qualified Secretary

and the custodian of the books and records and seal of   ,

a corporation duly formed pursuant to the laws of the State of   ,

and that the foregoing is a true record of a resolution duly adopted at a meeting of the

Board of Directors, and that said meeting was held in accordance with state law and the

Bylaws of the above-named Corporation on   ,   (year), and that

said resolution is now in full force and effect without modification or rescission.

IN WITNESS WHEREOF, I have executed my name as Secretary and have hereunto

affixed the corporate seal of the above-named Corporation this   day of   ,

          (year).

A True Record.

Attest.

_____
Secretary

RESOLUTION:
PURCHASE MOTOR VEHICLE

WHEREAS, an additional motor vehicle is necessary for the operation of the business; be it

RESOLVED, to purchase a motor vehicle described as

from   for the purchase price

of $.

The undersigned hereby certifies that he/she is the duly elected and qualified Secretary and the custodian of the books and records and seal of   , a corporation duly formed pursuant to the laws of the State of   , and that the foregoing is a true record of a resolution duly adopted at a meeting of the Board of Directors, and that said meeting was held in accordance with state law and the Bylaws of the above-named Corporation on   ,   (year), and that said resolution is now in full force and effect without modification or rescission.

IN WITNESS WHEREOF, I have executed my name as Secretary and have hereunto affixed the corporate seal of the above-named Corporation this   day of   ,

(year).

A True Record.

Attest.

_____
Secretary

RESOLUTION:
PURCHASE REAL ESTATE

WHEREAS, the Corporation requires additional facilities for the operation of its business, and

WHEREAS, it would be desirous to own rather than rent said premises; be it

RESOLVED, that the Corporation purchase and acquire real estate known or described

as   from

, for the purchase price of $, all as further set forth in a purchase and

sales agreement as annexed hereto.

The undersigned hereby certifies that he/she is the duly elected and qualified Secretary

and the custodian of the books and records and seal of   ,

a corporation duly formed pursuant to the laws of the State of   ,

and that the foregoing is a true record of a resolution duly adopted at a meeting of the

Board of Directors, and that said meeting was held in accordance with state law and the

Bylaws of the above-named Corporation on   ,   (year), and that

said resolution is now in full force and effect without modification or rescission.

IN WITNESS WHEREOF, I have executed my name as Secretary and have hereunto

affixed the corporate seal of the above-named Corporation this   day of   ,

    (year).

A True Record.

Attest.

_____
    Secretary

RESOLUTION:
QUALIFY AS A FOREIGN CORPORATION

WHEREAS, the Corporation has or shall conduct business within the state of

; be it

RESOLVED, to have the Corporation qualify as a foreign Corporation in the state of

.

The undersigned hereby certifies that he/she is the duly elected and qualified Secretary

and the custodian of the books and records and seal of   ,

a corporation duly formed pursuant to the laws of the State of   ,

and that the foregoing is a true record of a resolution duly adopted at a meeting of the

Board of Directors, and that said meeting was held in accordance with state law and the

Bylaws of the above-named Corporation on   ,   (year), and that

said resolution is now in full force and effect without modification or rescission.

IN WITNESS WHEREOF, I have executed my name as Secretary and have hereunto

affixed the corporate seal of the above-named Corporation this   day of   ,

(year).

A True Record.

Attest.

_____
Secretary

RESOLUTION:
RATIFY ACTS

WHEREAS,   , as   of the Corporation, has made a full report to the Board of Directors of all major matters and actions to which   has been a party; be it

RESOLVED, that the Board does hereby ratify and affirm each and every action undertaken by   , on behalf of the Corporation wherein said Board has knowledge of said act and wherein it has been fully and accurately stated.

The undersigned hereby certifies that he/she is the duly elected and qualified Secretary and the custodian of the books and records and seal of   , a corporation duly formed pursuant to the laws of the State of   , and that the foregoing is a true record of a resolution duly adopted at a meeting of the Board of Directors, and that said meeting was held in accordance with state law and the Bylaws of the above-named Corporation on   ,   (year), and that said resolution is now in full force and effect without modification or rescission.

IN WITNESS WHEREOF, I have executed my name as Secretary and have hereunto affixed the corporate seal of the above-named Corporation this   day of   ,   (year).

A True Record.

Attest.

_____
Secretary

RESOLUTION:
RATIFY BOARD OF DIRECTORS' ACTIONS

WHEREAS, all actions by the Board of Directors from   ,

(year), to   ,   (year), have been duly presented to the

shareholders at a shareholders meeting duly called and assembled; be it

RESOLVED, that the shareholders of the Corporation do hereby ratify and affirm all

actions of the Board as presented to the shareholders.

The undersigned hereby certifies that he/she is the duly elected and qualified Secretary

and the custodian of the books and records and seal of   ,

a corporation duly formed pursuant to the laws of the State of   ,

and that the foregoing is a true record of a resolution duly adopted at a meeting of the

Stockholders, and that said meeting was held in accordance with state law and the Bylaws

of the above-named Corporation on   ,   (year), and that said

resolution is now in full force and effect without modification or rescission.

IN WITNESS WHEREOF, I have executed my name as Secretary and have hereunto

affixed the corporate seal of the above-named Corporation this   day of   ,

(year).

A True Record.

Attest.

_____
                                                     Secretary

RESOLUTION:
REACQUIRE AND REDEEM OUTSTANDING SHARES

WHEREAS, the Board of Directors of this Corporation has determined that it is in the best interests of the Corporation to reacquire certain shares of stock from its stockholders, and to thereafter retire said shares as non-voting Treasury stock; be it

RESOLVED, that the Corporation hereby make an offer of redemption to its shareholders in accordance with the terms of offer as are annexed hereto; and

RESOLVED FURTHER, that the President of the Corporation undertake all actions necessary to carry out the foregoing resolution.

The undersigned hereby certifies that he/she is the duly elected and qualified Secretary and the custodian of the books and records and seal of   ,
a corporation duly formed pursuant to the laws of the State of   ,
and that the foregoing is a true record of a resolution duly adopted at a meeting of the Stockholders, and that said meeting was held in accordance with state law and the Bylaws of the above-named Corporation on   ,   (year), and that said resolution is now in full force and effect without modification or rescission.

IN WITNESS WHEREOF, I have executed my name as Secretary and have hereunto affixed the corporate seal of the above-named Corporation this   day of   ,
          (year).

A True Record.

Attest.

_____
Secretary

FORM R552

RESOLUTION:
REIMBURSE LENDER

RESOLVED, that the Corporation reimburse   the sum

of $ for monies paid by

in connection with the business of the Corporation, and more particularly:

The undersigned hereby certifies that he/she is the duly elected and qualified Secretary

and the custodian of the books and records and seal of   ,

a corporation duly formed pursuant to the laws of the State of   ,

and that the foregoing is a true record of a resolution duly adopted at a meeting of the

Board of Directors, and that said meeting was held in accordance with state law and the

Bylaws of the above-named Corporation on   ,   (year), and that

said resolution is now in full force and effect without modification or rescission.

IN WITNESS WHEREOF, I have executed my name as Secretary and have hereunto

affixed the corporate seal of the above-named Corporation this   day of   ,

        (year).

A True Record.

Attest.

_____
Secretary

RESOLUTION:
RETAIN ACCOUNTANT

WHEREAS, the Corporation requires the services of an accountant for general accounting purposes, including the preparation of tax returns; be it

RESOLVED, that the Corporation for its general accounting and tax needs retain the accounting firm of   , upon such terms as may be contained in the proposed terms of engagement annexed hereto or upon such generally prevailing rates as are customarily charged by said accountant.

The undersigned hereby certifies that he/she is the duly elected and qualified Secretary and the custodian of the books and records and seal of   ,
a corporation duly formed pursuant to the laws of the State of   ,
and that the foregoing is a true record of a resolution duly adopted at a meeting of the Board of Directors, and that said meeting was held in accordance with state law and the Bylaws of the above-named Corporation on   ,   (year), and that said resolution is now in full force and effect without modification or rescission.

IN WITNESS WHEREOF, I have executed my name as Secretary and have hereunto affixed the corporate seal of the above-named Corporation this   day of   ,
        (year).

A True Record.

Attest.

_____
Secretary

RESOLUTION:
RETAIN ATTORNEY

WHEREAS, the Corporation requires the services of an attorney for its general legal affairs; be it

RESOLVED, that the Corporation, for its general legal needs, appoint the law firm of

_____ as its general counsel; such appointment being further upon those terms as set forth in the proposed terms of engagements annexed hereto or upon such generally prevailing rates as are customarily charged by said attorney.

The undersigned hereby certifies that he/she is the duly elected and qualified Secretary and the custodian of the books and records and seal of   ,

a corporation duly formed pursuant to the laws of the State of   ,

and that the foregoing is a true record of a resolution duly adopted at a meeting of the Board of Directors, and that said meeting was held in accordance with state law and the Bylaws of the above-named Corporation on   ,   (year), and that said resolution is now in full force and effect without modification or rescission.

IN WITNESS WHEREOF, I have executed my name as Secretary and have hereunto affixed the corporate seal of the above-named Corporation this   day of   ,

            (year).

A True Record.

Attest.

_____
Secretary

RESOLUTION:
RETAIN BUSINESS BROKER

WHEREAS, the Corporation desires to sell its business, and

WHEREAS, the Corporation desires to retain a licensed business broker for said purpose; be it

RESOLVED, that the Corporation retain   as its business broker for purposes of selling the business, said terms of appointment being as contained in a listing agreement annexed hereto.

The undersigned hereby certifies that he/she is the duly elected and qualified Secretary and the custodian of the books and records and seal of   , a corporation duly formed pursuant to the laws of the State of   , and that the foregoing is a true record of a resolution duly adopted at a meeting of the Board of Directors, and that said meeting was held in accordance with state law and the Bylaws of the above-named Corporation on   ,   (year), and that said resolution is now in full force and effect without modification or rescission.

IN WITNESS WHEREOF, I have executed my name as Secretary and have hereunto affixed the corporate seal of the above-named Corporation this   day of   ,   (year).

A True Record.

Attest.

_____
Secretary

RESOLUTION:
RETAIN CONSULTANT

WHEREAS, the Corporation requires professional assistance in the area of:

                                                ; be it

RESOLVED, that the Corporation retain   as a business consultant for the above general purposes and that the terms of engagement shall be as contained in the consultant agreement annexed hereto.

The undersigned hereby certifies that he/she is the duly elected and qualified Secretary and the custodian of the books and records and seal of   , a corporation duly formed pursuant to the laws of the State of   , and that the foregoing is a true record of a resolution duly adopted at a meeting of the Board of Directors, and that said meeting was held in accordance with state law and the Bylaws of the above-named Corporation on   ,   (year), and that said resolution is now in full force and effect without modification or rescission.

IN WITNESS WHEREOF, I have executed my name as Secretary and have hereunto affixed the corporate seal of the above-named Corporation this   day of   ,   (year).

A True Record.

Attest.

_____
Secretary

RESOLUTION:
RETAIN REAL ESTATE BROKER

WHEREAS, the Corporation is desirous of selling certain real estate, and

WHEREAS, the Corporation desires to retain a licensed real estate broker for that purpose; be it

RESOLVED, that the Corporation retain   as its real estate broker for purposes of selling certain real estate owned by the Corporation known as

                                , said terms of appointment as are contained in the broker's agreement annexed hereto.

The undersigned hereby certifies that he/she is the duly elected and qualified Secretary and the custodian of the books and records and seal of   ,
a corporation duly formed pursuant to the laws of the State of   ,
and that the foregoing is a true record of a resolution duly adopted at a meeting of the Board of Directors, and that said meeting was held in accordance with state law and the Bylaws of the above-named Corporation on   ,   (year), and that said resolution is now in full force and effect without modification or rescission.

IN WITNESS WHEREOF, I have executed my name as Secretary and have hereunto affixed the corporate seal of the above-named Corporation this   day of   ,
        (year).

A True Record.

Attest.

_____

Secretary

RESOLUTION:
RETAIN SPECIAL ACCOUNTANT

WHEREAS, the Corporation has need of an accountant for the specific purpose of:

; be it

RESOLVED, to appoint   accountant for said purposes and all matters incidental to said purpose.

Said accountant shall be compensated in accordance with his generally prevailing rates.

The undersigned hereby certifies that he/she is the duly elected and qualified Secretary and the custodian of the books and records and seal of   , a corporation duly formed pursuant to the laws of the State of   , and that the foregoing is a true record of a resolution duly adopted at a meeting of the Board of Directors, and that said meeting was held in accordance with state law and the Bylaws of the above-named Corporation on   ,   (year), and that said resolution is now in full force and effect without modification or rescission.

IN WITNESS WHEREOF, I have executed my name as Secretary and have hereunto affixed the corporate seal of the above-named Corporation this   day of   , (year).

A True Record.

Attest.

_____
Secretary

RESOLUTION:
RETAIN SPECIAL ATTORNEY

WHEREAS, the Corporation has need for an attorney solely for the specific purpose of:

; be it

RESOLVED, that the Corporation retain   as

special counsel solely for the aforesaid purpose and all matters incidental thereto and that

said counsel shall be compensated in accordance with his generally prevailing rates.

The undersigned hereby certifies that he/she is the duly elected and qualified Secretary

and the custodian of the books and records and seal of   ,

a corporation duly formed pursuant to the laws of the State of   ,

and that the foregoing is a true record of a resolution duly adopted at a meeting of the

Board of Directors, and that said meeting was held in accordance with state law and the

Bylaws of the above-named Corporation on   ,   (year), and that

said resolution is now in full force and effect without modification or rescission.

IN WITNESS WHEREOF, I have executed my name as Secretary and have hereunto

affixed the corporate seal of the above-named Corporation this   day of   ,

(year).

A True Record.

Attest.

_____
Secretary

FORM R560

RESOLUTION:
SELL ASSETS SUBJECT TO SHAREHOLDER APPROVAL

WHEREAS, an offer has been made to this Corporation by

to purchase the entire assets of this Corporation for the consideration and upon the terms and conditions set forth in the proposed agreement as annexed, and

WHEREAS, in the opinion of this Board of Directors, it is in the best interests of this Corporation that its entire assets be sold to

upon the price, terms and conditions in the proposed agreement above, be it

RESOLVED, that the offer of said   is hereby accepted, subject to the approval of the stockholders of this Corporation, and

RESOLVED FURTHER, that the President and the Secretary are hereby authorized and directed to make, execute, and deliver the aforementioned agreement upon the adoption of the same by the stockholders of this Corporation, and

RESOLVED FURTHER, that the Secretary of the Corporation notice a special stockholder meeting for the purposes of obtaining stockholder approval to said sale.

The undersigned hereby certifies that he/she is the duly elected and qualified Secretary

and the custodian of the books and records and seal of   ,

a corporation duly formed pursuant to the laws of the State of   ,

and that the foregoing is a true record of a resolution duly adopted at a meeting of the

Board of Directors, and that said meeting was held in accordance with state law and the

Bylaws of the above-named Corporation on   ,   (year), and that

said resolution is now in full force and effect without modification or rescission.

IN WITNESS WHEREOF, I have executed my name as Secretary and have hereunto affixed the corporate seal of the above-named Corporation this   day of   ,

(year).

A True Record.

Attest.

_____
Secretary

RESOLUTION:
SELL BUSINESS ASSETS

WHEREAS, the Corporation has received an offer from

to purchase all the assets of the Corporation as a going business concern, all as were particularly set forth in a purchase agreement annexed hereto; and

WHEREAS, in the opinion of the Board, it is in the best interests of the Corporation and its shareholders for the Corporation to sell its assets pursuant to the terms of agreement; be it

RESOLVED, that the offer to purchase the assets of the Corporation is hereby accepted by the Board, but subject to approval and ratification by the requisite number of shareholders of the Corporation; and

RESOLVED FURTHER, that upon shareholder approval, the President of the Corporation undertake all acts and execute all documents as necessary to consummate said transaction upon its terms.

The undersigned hereby certifies that he/she is the duly elected and qualified Secretary and the custodian of the books and records and seal of   ,

a corporation duly formed pursuant to the laws of the State of   ,

and that the foregoing is a true record of a resolution duly adopted at a meeting of the Stockholders, and that said meeting was held in accordance with state law and the Bylaws of the above-named Corporation on   ,   (year), and that said resolution is now in full force and effect without modification or rescission.

IN WITNESS WHEREOF, I have executed my name as Secretary and have hereunto affixed the corporate seal of the above-named Corporation this   day of   ,

(year).

A True Record.

Attest.

_____
Secretary

RESOLUTION:
SELL CORPORATE SHARES

WHEREAS, _____ has duly subscribed for

(_____) shares of the common stock for the aggregate subscription price of

$ _____ , and

WHEREAS, the Board of Directors deems it to be in the best interests of the Corporation

to accept said subscription; be it

RESOLVED, that the Corporation does hereby accept the stock subscription of

_____ , to purchase (_____) shares of the Corporation for $ _____

, and, it is

RESOLVED FURTHER, that upon tender of the subscription price, the Treasurer of the

Corporation issue to _____ , or his or her nominee, (_____) shares

of the no-par value common stock.

The undersigned hereby certifies that he/she is the duly elected and qualified Secretary

and the custodian of the books and records and seal of _____ ,

a corporation duly formed pursuant to the laws of the State of _____ ,

and that the foregoing is a true record of a resolution duly adopted at a meeting of the

Stockholders, and that said meeting was held in accordance with state law and the Bylaws

of the above-named Corporation on _____ , _____ (year), and that said

resolution is now in full force and effect without modification or rescission.

IN WITNESS WHEREOF, I have executed my name as Secretary and have hereunto

affixed the corporate seal of the above-named Corporation this _____ day of _____ ,

_____ (year).

A True Record.

Attest.

_____
Secretary

RESOLUTION:
SELL EQUIPMENT

WHEREAS, certain equipment owned by the Corporation is no longer necessary for its operation; be it

RESOLVED, to sell certain equipment described as

to   for the sales

price of $.

The undersigned hereby certifies that he/she is the duly elected and qualified Secretary and the custodian of the books and records and seal of   , a corporation duly formed pursuant to the laws of the State of   , and that the foregoing is a true record of a resolution duly adopted at a meeting of the Stockholders, and that said meeting was held in accordance with state law and the Bylaws of the above-named Corporation on   ,   (year), and that said resolution is now in full force and effect without modification or rescission.

IN WITNESS WHEREOF, I have executed my name as Secretary and have hereunto affixed the corporate seal of the above-named Corporation this   day of   ,

        (year).

A True Record.

Attest.

_____

Secretary

RESOLUTION:
SELL MOTOR VEHICLE

WHEREAS, a certain motor vehicle owned by the Corporation is no longer necessary for the proper operation of the business; be it

RESOLVED, to sell a certain motor vehicle described as

                                                to   for the sales price of $.

The undersigned hereby certifies that he/she is the duly elected and qualified Secretary and the custodian of the books and records and seal of   , a corporation duly formed pursuant to the laws of the State of   , and that the foregoing is a true record of a resolution duly adopted at a meeting of the Board of Directors, and that said meeting was held in accordance with state law and the Bylaws of the above-named Corporation on   ,   (year), and that said resolution is now in full force and effect without modification or rescission.

IN WITNESS WHEREOF, I have executed my name as Secretary and have hereunto affixed the corporate seal of the above-named Corporation this   day of   ,   (year).

A True Record.

Attest.

_____
Secretary

RESOLUTION:
SELL REAL ESTATE

WHEREAS, the Corporation owns certain real estate that is no longer needed for the operation of the business and that it would further be desirous to sell some; be it

RESOLVED, that the Corporation sell real estate known or described as

to

for the purchase price of $, all as set forth in a certain purchase and sales agreement as annexed hereto.

The undersigned hereby certifies that he/she is the duly elected and qualified Secretary and the custodian of the books and records and seal of   ,
a corporation duly formed pursuant to the laws of the State of   ,
and that the foregoing is a true record of a resolution duly adopted at a meeting of the Board of Directors, and that said meeting was held in accordance with state law and the Bylaws of the above-named Corporation on   ,   (year), and that said resolution is now in full force and effect without modification or rescission.

IN WITNESS WHEREOF, I have executed my name as Secretary and have hereunto affixed the corporate seal of the above-named Corporation this   day of   ,
        (year).

A True Record.

Attest.

_____
Secretary

RESOLUTION:
SETTLE LITIGATION

WHEREAS, the Corporation and   are presently engaged in litigation, and

WHEREAS, an offer of settlement has been proposed, and

WHEREAS, it is in the best interests of the Corporation to accept said settlement and terminate the litigation; be it

RESOLVED, that the Corporation accept the settlement offer as presented to the Board and as set forth in offer of settlement annexed; and, it is

RESOLVED FURTHER, that the President of the Corporation, together with counsel, be authorized to execute and deliver all documents and undertake such acts as are necessary to comply with the terms of settlement.

The undersigned hereby certifies that he/she is the duly elected and qualified Secretary and the custodian of the books and records and seal of   , a corporation duly formed pursuant to the laws of the State of   , and that the foregoing is a true record of a resolution duly adopted at a meeting of the Board of Directors, and that said meeting was held in accordance with state law and the Bylaws of the above-named Corporation on   ,   (year), and that said resolution is now in full force and effect without modification or rescission.

IN WITNESS WHEREOF, I have executed my name as Secretary and have hereunto affixed the corporate seal of the above-named Corporation this   day of   ,
         (year).

A True Record.

Attest.

_____
Secretary

RESOLUTION:
SUBLET SPACE

WHEREAS, the Corporation holds certain space that is no longer required for the efficient operation of its business; be it

RESOLVED, that the Corporation sublet certain space at

to

; said sublet commencing on   ,   (year), and further subject to the terms and conditions of a certain sublet agreement as annexed hereto.

The undersigned hereby certifies that he/she is the duly elected and qualified Secretary and the custodian of the books and records and seal of   ,

a corporation duly formed pursuant to the laws of the State of   ,

and that the foregoing is a true record of a resolution duly adopted at a meeting of the Board of Directors, and that said meeting was held in accordance with state law and the Bylaws of the above-named Corporation on   ,   (year), and that said resolution is now in full force and effect without modification or rescission.

IN WITNESS WHEREOF, I have executed my name as Secretary and have hereunto affixed the corporate seal of the above-named Corporation this   day of   ,

(year).

A True Record.

Attest.

_____
Secretary

RESOLUTION:
TERMINATE CONTRACT

WHEREAS, the Corporation and

are presently parties to a contract dated   ,   (year), whereby said

contract summarily calls for:

                                                                                                              ,

and

WHEREAS, the Corporation deems it to be in the best interests of both parties to

terminate said contract as to any non-performed part thereon; be it

RESOLVED, that the Corporation herewith terminate said contract on the terms

contained as annexed hereto.

The undersigned hereby certifies that he/she is the duly elected and qualified Secretary

and the custodian of the books and records and seal of   ,

a corporation duly formed pursuant to the laws of the State of   ,

and that the foregoing is a true record of a resolution duly adopted at a meeting of the

Board of Directors, and that said meeting was held in accordance with state law and the

Bylaws of the above-named Corporation on   ,   (year), and that

said resolution is now in full force and effect without modification or rescission.

IN WITNESS WHEREOF, I have executed my name as Secretary and have hereunto

affixed the corporate seal of the above-named Corporation this   day of   ,

          (year).

A True Record.

Attest.

_____
Secretary

RESOLUTION:
TERMINATE EMPLOYEE

WHEREAS,   in his capacity as

, has not fulfilled his responsibilities adequately; be it

RESOLVED, that   's employment with the Corporation

be terminated as of   ,   (year), and that

be provided the customary severance pay and benefits.

The undersigned hereby certifies that he/she is the duly elected and qualified Secretary

and the custodian of the books and records and seal of   ,

a corporation duly formed pursuant to the laws of the State of   ,

and that the foregoing is a true record of a resolution duly adopted at a meeting of the

Board of Directors, and that said meeting was held in accordance with state law and the

Bylaws of the above-named Corporation on   ,   (year), and that

said resolution is now in full force and effect without modification or rescission.

IN WITNESS WHEREOF, I have executed my name as Secretary and have hereunto

affixed the corporate seal of the above-named Corporation this   day of   ,

       (year).

A True Record.

Attest.

_____
Secretary

RESOLUTION:
TERMINATE LEASE

WHEREAS, the Corporation has no further need for certain space that it occupies as a tenant; be it

RESOLVED, to terminate as tenant a certain lease from   , as landlord, said lease dated   ,   (year), for premises at

. The termination date shall be   ,   (year), with surrender of the premises by the Corporation on or before said date.

The undersigned hereby certifies that he/she is the duly elected and qualified Secretary and the custodian of the books and records and seal of   , a corporation duly formed pursuant to the laws of the State of   and that the foregoing is a true record of a resolution duly adopted at a meeting of the Board of Directors, and that said meeting was held in accordance with state law and the Bylaws of the above-named Corporation on   ,   (year), and that said resolution is now in full force and effect without modification or rescission.

IN WITNESS WHEREOF, I have executed my name as Secretary and have hereunto affixed the corporate seal of the above-named Corporation this   day of   , (year).

A True Record.

Attest.

_____
Secretary

RESOLUTION:
WAIVE RESTRICTIONS ON TRANSFER

RESOLVED, to waive all restrictions of transfer imposed on the shares of stock of the Corporation for purposes of allowing a transfer of   (   ) shares of common stock of the Corporation from   to   , provided that said restrictions shall apply to any further transfer of said shares.

The undersigned hereby certifies that he/she is the duly elected and qualified Secretary and the custodian of the books and records and seal of   , a corporation duly formed pursuant to the laws of the State of   , and that the foregoing is a true record of a resolution duly adopted at a meeting of the Stockholders, and that said meeting was held in accordance with state law and the Bylaws of the above-named Corporation on   ,   (year), and that said resolution is now in full force and effect without modification or rescission.

IN WITNESS WHEREOF, I have executed my name as Secretary and have hereunto affixed the corporate seal of the above-named Corporation this   day of   , (year).).

A True Record.

Attest.

_____
Secretary

Dividends

Chapter 6
Dividends

Forms in this chapter:

DIRECTOR'S DISSENT TO BOARD ACTION

Mr./Ms.

Secretary

Dear Sir/Madam:

In my capacity as a director of _____, I hereby notify you of my dissent from the action taken by the Board of Directors of _____, at its meeting on _____, _____ (year), from which I was absent. The action I dissent from was the board's decision to:

I hereby request that you enter my dissent in the minutes of the meeting of _____, _____ (year), of the Board of Directors, and that you advise each member of the board of this request.

Sincerely,

_____

Director

RESOLUTION:
APPOINT APPRAISER TO APPRAISE ASSETS

WHEREAS, the board has reason to believe that certain assets are carried on the books for an amount not consistent with their true worth; be it

RESOLVED, that the Corporation retain a professional appraiser for purposes of valuing the following described assets of the Corporation:

The undersigned hereby certifies that he/she is the duly elected and qualified Secretary and the custodian of the books and records and seal of   ,

a corporation duly formed pursuant to the laws of the state of   ,

and that the foregoing is a true record of a resolution duly adopted at a meeting of the Board of Directors, and that said meeting was held in accordance with state law and the Bylaws of the above-named Corporation on   ,   (year), and that said resolution is now in full force and effect without modification or rescission.

IN WITNESS WHEREOF, I have executed my name as Secretary and have hereunto affixed the corporate seal of the above-named Corporation this   day of   ,

        (year).

A True Record.

Attest.

_____
Secretary

RESOLUTION:
APPROVE LOAN TO PAY DIVIDEND

WHEREAS, the Corporation has accumulated a surplus sufficient to pay the declared dividend of   percent on the common stock payable on   ,
(year), to stockholders of record at the close of business on   ,
(year), and

WHEREAS, the cash surplus can be more advantageously used for the expansion of the business, be it

RESOLVED, that the President is hereby authorized to transact a loan from
                          Bank for the amount of the dividend declared, and

RESOLVED FURTHER, that, upon obtaining the said loan, the Treasurer is hereby directed and authorized to pay out from the fund so borrowed the declared dividend on the date specified.

The undersigned hereby certifies that he/she is the duly elected and qualified Secretary and the custodian of the books and records and seal of   ,
a corporation duly formed pursuant to the laws of the state of   ,
and that the foregoing is a true record of a resolution duly adopted at a meeting of the Board of Directors, and that said meeting was held in accordance with state law and the Bylaws of the above-named Corporation on   ,   (year), and that said resolution is now in full force and effect without modification or rescission.

IN WITNESS WHEREOF, I have executed my name as Secretary and have hereunto affixed the corporate seal of the above-named Corporation this   day of   ,
(year).

A True Record.

Attest.

_____
Secretary

RESOLUTION:
AUTHORIZE ADDITIONAL CASH DIVIDEND

WHEREAS, there are sufficient surplus net earnings of this Corporation to justify the declaration of a larger than customary dividend; be it

RESOLVED, that an additional dividend of   percent is herewith declared upon the common stock of the Corporation, payable on   ,   (year), to stockholders of record at the close of business on   ,   (year).

The undersigned hereby certifies that he/she is the duly elected and qualified Secretary and the custodian of the books and records and seal of   , a corporation duly formed pursuant to the laws of the state of   , and that the foregoing is a true record of a resolution duly adopted at a meeting of the Board of Directors, and that said meeting was held in accordance with state law and the Bylaws of the above-named Corporation on   ,   (year), and that said resolution is now in full force and effect without modification or rescission.

IN WITNESS WHEREOF, I have executed my name as Secretary and have hereunto affixed the corporate seal of the above-named Corporation this   day of   ,   (year).

A True Record.

Attest.

_____
Secretary

RESOLUTION:
AUTHORIZE CASH DIVIDEND

WHEREAS, the Corporation has an accumulated earned surplus of $ as

of   ,   (year), and

WHEREAS, the board has determined that a cash dividend can be payable to

shareholders; be it

RESOLVED, that the Corporation issue a quarterly dividend declared payable to

shareholders of record of the common stock, as of   ,   (year), in

the amount of $ per share, and

FURTHER RESOLVED, that the treasurer may pay said dividends from the general

accounts of the Corporation.

The undersigned hereby certifies that he/she is the duly elected and qualified Secretary

and the custodian of the books and records and seal of   ,

a corporation duly formed pursuant to the laws of the state of   ,

and that the foregoing is a true record of a resolution duly adopted at a meeting of the

Board of Directors, and that said meeting was held in accordance with state law and the

Bylaws of the above-named Corporation on   ,   (year), and that

said resolution is now in full force and effect without modification or rescission.

IN WITNESS WHEREOF, I have executed my name as Secretary and have hereunto

affixed the corporate seal of the above-named Corporation this   day of   ,

     (year).

A True Record.

Attest.

_____
Secretary

RESOLUTION:
DECLARE AN EXTRA DIVIDEND

RESOLVED, that the regular dividend of

dollars ($) per share shall be supplemented by an additional payment of

dollars ($) per

share so that the total amount of the regular dividend and the extra dividend shall be

dollars ($) per share, and

the Treasurer is hereby authorized and directed to set aside a sufficient portion of the

current surplus to satisfy such dividend payment, and the Treasurer is further directed to

make such dividend payable to all shareholders of record at the close of business on the

day of   ,   (year).

The undersigned hereby certifies that he/she is the duly elected and qualified Secretary

and the custodian of the books and records and seal of   ,

a corporation duly formed pursuant to the laws of the state of   ,

and that the foregoing is a true record of a resolution duly adopted at a meeting of the

Board of Directors, and that said meeting was held in accordance with state law and the

Bylaws of the above-named Corporation on   ,   (year), and that

said resolution is now in full force and effect without modification or rescission.

IN WITNESS WHEREOF, I have executed my name as Secretary and have hereunto

affixed the corporate seal of the above-named Corporation this   day of   ,

(year).

A True Record.

Attest.

_____
Secretary

RESOLUTION:
OMIT A DIVIDEND

RESOLVED, that a regular dividend will not be declared on the common stock of this Corporation for the   quarter of   ,   (year), and that the amount so saved is to be retained by the Corporation in its surplus account.

The undersigned hereby certifies that he/she is the duly elected and qualified Secretary and the custodian of the books and records and seal of   , a corporation duly formed pursuant to the laws of the state of   , and that the foregoing is a true record of a resolution duly adopted at a meeting of the Board of Directors, and that said meeting was held in accordance with state law and the Bylaws of the above-named Corporation on   ,   (year), and that said resolution is now in full force and effect without modification or rescission.

IN WITNESS WHEREOF, I have executed my name as Secretary and have hereunto affixed the corporate seal of the above-named Corporation this   day of   , (year).

A True Record.

Attest.

_____
Secretary

RESOLUTION:
RETAIN EARNINGS

WHEREAS, the Corporation has an earned surplus from which dividends can be paid, but that preservation of said surplus is necessary to improve the Corporation's financial condition; be it

RESOLVED, that no dividends be declared for the _____ ending _____ , _____ (year), and that the accumulated earnings be added to the surplus account of the Corporation.

The undersigned hereby certifies that he/she is the duly elected and qualified Secretary and the custodian of the books and records and seal of _____ , a corporation duly formed pursuant to the laws of the state of _____ , and that the foregoing is a true record of a resolution duly adopted at a meeting of the Board of Directors, and that said meeting was held in accordance with state law and the Bylaws of the above-named Corporation on _____ , _____ (year), and that said resolution is now in full force and effect without modification or rescission.

IN WITNESS WHEREOF, I have executed my name as Secretary and have hereunto affixed the corporate seal of the above-named Corporation this _____ day of _____ , _____ (year).

A True Record.

Attest.

_____
Secretary

RESOLUTION:
STATE CORPORATION'S DIVIDEND POLICY

RESOLVED, that it is this Corporation's dividend policy to pay a dividend of

dollars ($) per

annum on the common stock of the Corporation, payable in quarterly installments on the

first day of ,   ,

and , if (1) the earnings of the

Corporation support such payments under the laws of the State of

, and (2) it is determined that the payment of such dividends is in the best interests of the

Corporation.

The undersigned hereby certifies that he/she is the duly elected and qualified Secretary

and the custodian of the books and records and seal of ,

a corporation duly formed pursuant to the laws of the state of ,

and that the foregoing is a true record of a resolution duly adopted at a meeting of the

Board of Directors, and that said meeting was held in accordance with state law and the

Bylaws of the above-named Corporation on ,   (year), and that

said resolution is now in full force and effect without modification or rescission.

IN WITNESS WHEREOF, I have executed my name as Secretary and have hereunto

affixed the corporate seal of the above-named Corporation this   day of ,

(year).

A True Record.

Attest.

_____

Secretary

Compensation and benefits

7

Chapter 7

Compensation and benefits

Forms in this chapter:

RESOLUTION:
ADOPT A SEVERANCE BENEFIT PLAN

WHEREAS, the Board of Directors of this Corporation deems it to be in the best interests of the Corporation and certain key employees to increase their pension contribution limit by establishing a Severance Benefit Plan under Section 419 (A) of the Internal Revenue Code; be it

RESOLVED, that the Corporation adopt a Severance Benefit Plan under Section 419 (A), all as set forth on the proposed plan as annexed; and, be it

RESOLVED FURTHER, that the President and/or Treasurer of the Corporation undertake all actions deemed necessary to implement and administer said plan.

The undersigned hereby certifies that he/she is the duly elected and qualified Secretary and the custodian of the books and records and seal of   , a corporation duly formed pursuant to the laws of the State of   , and that the foregoing is a true record of a resolution duly adopted at a meeting of the Board of Directors, and that said meeting was held in accordance with state law and the Bylaws of the above-named Corporation on   ,   (year), and that said resolution is now in full force and effect without modification or rescission.

IN WITNESS WHEREOF, I have executed my name as Secretary and have hereunto affixed the corporate seal of the above-named Corporation this   day of   ,

(year).

A True Record.

Attest.

_____
Secretary

RESOLUTION:
ADOPT CAFETERIA PLAN OF BENEFITS

WHEREAS, the Board of Directors has determined that it would be in the best interests of the Corporation and its employees to adopt a "Cafeteria Plan" of fringe benefits, so-called; be it

RESOLVED, that the Corporation adopt a so-called "Cafeteria Plan" of benefits to its employees, all in accordance with the specifications annexed hereto; and, be it

RESOLVED FURTHER, that the President and/or Treasurer of the Corporation undertake all actions necessary to implement and administer said plan.

The undersigned hereby certifies that he/she is the duly elected and qualified Secretary and the custodian of the books and records and seal of _____ , a corporation duly formed pursuant to the laws of the State of _____ , and that the foregoing is a true record of a resolution duly adopted at a meeting of the Board of Directors, and that said meeting was held in accordance with state law and the Bylaws of the above-named Corporation on _____ , _____ (year), and that said resolution is now in full force and effect without modification or rescission.

IN WITNESS WHEREOF, I have executed my name as Secretary and have hereunto affixed the corporate seal of the above-named Corporation this _____ day of _____ , (year).

A True Record.

Attest.

_____
Secretary

RESOLUTION:
ADOPT EMPLOYEE BENEFIT PLAN

WHEREAS, it shall improve employee morale and aid in the recruitment of new employees and retention of existing employees if the Corporation establish an Employee Benefit Plan (Plan), and

WHEREAS, the Board of Directors has considered the Plan as annexed and believes it to be in the best interests of the Corporation to adopt; be it

RESOLVED, that the Board of Directors approves the adoption of the Plan as annexed hereto, and subject to further approval and ratification of same by the shareholders with requisite voting powers, and be it

RESOLVED FURTHER, that upon shareholder approval, the officers of the Corporation undertake all actions necessary to implement the Plan.

The undersigned hereby certifies that he/she is the duly elected and qualified Secretary and the custodian of the books and records and seal of   ,
a corporation duly formed pursuant to the laws of the State of   ,
and that the foregoing is a true record of a resolution duly adopted at a meeting of the Board of Directors, and that said meeting was held in accordance with state law and the Bylaws of the above-named Corporation on   ,   (year), and that said resolution is now in full force and effect without modification or rescission.

IN WITNESS WHEREOF, I have executed my name as Secretary and have hereunto affixed the corporate seal of the above-named Corporation this   day of   ,
        (year).

A True Record.

Attest.

_____
Secretary

RESOLUTION:
ADOPT EMPLOYEE WELFARE PLAN

WHEREAS, the Board of Directors of this Corporation has deemed it advisable to adopt an Employee Welfare Plan to provide for the general welfare of its employees; be it

RESOLVED, that this Corporation adopt an Employee Welfare Plan in accordance with the provisions and specifications as have been presented to and reviewed by this Board, a copy of which is annexed hereto; and, be it

RESOLVED FURTHER, that the President and/or Treasurer of this Corporation undertake such action as is necessary to implement and administer said plan.

The undersigned hereby certifies that he/she is the duly elected and qualified Secretary and the custodian of the books and records and seal of   , a corporation duly formed pursuant to the laws of the State of   and that the foregoing is a true record of a resolution duly adopted at a meeting of the Board of Directors, and that said meeting was held in accordance with state law and the Bylaws of the above-named Corporation on   ,   (year), and that said resolution is now in full force and effect without modification or rescission.

IN WITNESS WHEREOF, I have executed my name as Secretary and have hereunto affixed the corporate seal of the above-named Corporation this   day of   ,   (year).

A True Record.

Attest.

_____
Secretary

RESOLUTION:
ADOPT WAGE CONTINUATION PLAN

WHEREAS, the officers of this Corporation, after careful deliberation, considered a plan providing for wage payments to sick and injured employees, and

WHEREAS, the officers have presented to this meeting their recommendation for the adoption of a Wage Continuation Plan, a copy of which is attached to and made a part of this Resolution, be it

RESOLVED, that the Board of Directors hereby adopts the attached Wage Continuation Plan, and that the Treasurer of this Corporation is hereby authorized and directed to make payments to eligible employees in accordance with said Plan.

The undersigned hereby certifies that he/she is the duly elected and qualified Secretary and the custodian of the books and records and seal of   ,
a corporation duly formed pursuant to the laws of the State of   ,
and that the foregoing is a true record of a resolution duly adopted at a meeting of the Board of Directors, and that said meeting was held in accordance with state law and the Bylaws of the above-named Corporation on   ,   (year), and that said resolution is now in full force and effect without modification or rescision.

IN WITNESS WHEREOF, I have executed my name as Secretary and have hereunto affixed the corporate seal of the above-named Corporation this   day of   ,
      (year).

A True Record.

Attest.

_____

Secretary

RESOLUTION:
APPROVE A 401K RETIREMENT PLAN

WHEREAS, the Board of Directors of the Corporation deems it to be in the best interests of the Corporation and its employees to establish a so-called 401 (K) qualified cash and deferred retirement arrangement (CODA) for its employees; be it

RESOLVED, that the Corporation adopt the proposed 401 (K) plan as is annexed hereto, conditional, however, upon counsel for the Corporation obtaining from the IRS a favorable ruling that said plan qualifies as a qualified-defined benefit plan; and

RESOLVED FURTHER, that upon satisfaction of the foregoing condition, the President and/or Treasurer of the Corporation undertake all actions necessary to implement and administer said plan.

The undersigned hereby certifies that he/she is the duly elected and qualified Secretary and the custodian of the books and records and seal of   ,
a corporation duly formed pursuant to the laws of the State of   ,
and that the foregoing is a true record of a resolution duly adopted at a meeting of the Board of Directors, and that said meeting was held in accordance with state law and the Bylaws of the above-named Corporation on   ,   (year), and that said resolution is now in full force and effect without modification or rescission.

IN WITNESS WHEREOF, I have executed my name as Secretary and have hereunto affixed the corporate seal of the above-named Corporation this   day of   ,
(year).

A True Record.

Attest.

_____
Secretary

RESOLUTION:
APPROVE A SIMPLIFIED EMPLOYEE PENSION PLAN

WHEREAS, the Board of Directors deems it advisable to establish a Simplified Employee Pension Plan (SEP) on behalf of its employees, whereby the Corporation shall make contributions to the IRA accounts of its employees; be it

RESOLVED, that the Corporation establish and administer for its employees a Simplified Employee Pension Plan (SEP, so-called) pursuant to Internal Revenue regulations and as further specified on the proposed plan, annexed, and be it

RESOLVED FURTHER, that the President and/or Treasurer undertake all actions necessary to implement and administer said plan.

The undersigned hereby certifies that he/she is the duly elected and qualified Secretary and the custodian of the books and records and seal of   ,
a corporation duly formed pursuant to the laws of the State of   ,
and that the foregoing is a true record of a resolution duly adopted at a meeting of the Board of Directors, and that said meeting was held in accordance with state law and the Bylaws of the above-named Corporation on   ,   (year), and that said resolution is now in full force and effect without modification or rescission.

IN WITNESS WHEREOF, I have executed my name as Secretary and have hereunto affixed the corporate seal of the above-named Corporation this   day of   ,
        (year).

A True Record.

Attest.

_____
Secretary

RESOLUTION:
APPROVE CASH BONUS

WHEREAS, in recognition of the fact that

has performed meritoriously on behalf of the Corporation and has through diligent effort

materially improved the profits of the Corporation, be it

RESOLVED, that said   be paid a cash bonus of

$ in addition to the regular compensation, and that said bonus be paid

as soon as practicable in the discretion of the Treasurer.

The undersigned hereby certifies that he/she is the duly elected and qualified Secretary

and the custodian of the books and records and seal of   ,

a corporation duly formed pursuant to the laws of the State of   ,

and that the foregoing is a true record of a resolution duly adopted at a meeting of the

Board of Directors, and that said meeting was held in accordance with state law and the

Bylaws of the above-named Corporation on   ,   (year), and that

said resolution is now in full force and effect without modification or rescission.

IN WITNESS WHEREOF, I have executed my name as Secretary and have hereunto

affixed the corporate seal of the above-named Corporation this   day of   ,

(year).

A True Record.

Attest.

_____

Secretary

RESOLUTION:
APPROVE EMPLOYEE LOAN PROGRAM

WHEREAS, the Board of Directors deems it advisable to institute a loan program for purposes of advancing loans to employees of the Corporation who will use said loan proceeds for purposes of advancing their own education or the education of their children; and

WHEREAS, the Board wishes to adopt a specific policy for said loan program benefit; be it

RESOLVED, that the Corporation adopt an Educational Loan Plan in accordance with the specification for said program as presented to the Board and annexed hereto, and, it is

RESOLVED FURTHER, that the President and/or Treasurer of the Corporation take all action necessary to implement and administer said plan.

The undersigned hereby certifies that he/she is the duly elected and qualified Secretary and the custodian of the books and records and seal of   ,
a corporation duly formed pursuant to the laws of the State of   ,
and that the foregoing is a true record of a resolution duly adopted at a meeting of the Board of Directors, and that said meeting was held in accordance with state law and the Bylaws of the above-named Corporation on   ,   (year), and that said resolution is now in full force and effect without modification or rescission.

IN WITNESS WHEREOF, I have executed my name as Secretary and have hereunto affixed the corporate seal of the above-named Corporation this   day of   ,
     (year).

A True Record.

Attest.

_____
Secretary

RESOLUTION:
APPROVE EMPLOYEE SCHOLARSHIP BENEFITS

WHEREAS, this Board of Directors deems it advisable for the Corporation to institute a program whereby eligible children of employees of the Corporation can obtain from the Corporation award scholarships to be used in the furtherance of their education; be it

RESOLVED, the Board adopts a certain Scholarship Aid Program in accordance with the specifications of said program as presented to the Board and annexed hereto; and, be it

RESOLVED FURTHER, that the President and/or Treasurer of the Corporation undertake all actions necessary to implement and administer said program.

The undersigned hereby certifies that he/she is the duly elected and qualified Secretary and the custodian of the books and records and seal of   ,
a corporation duly formed pursuant to the laws of the State of   ,
and that the foregoing is a true record of a resolution duly adopted at a meeting of the Board of Directors, and that said meeting was held in accordance with state law and the Bylaws of the above-named Corporation on   ,   (year), and that said resolution is now in full force and effect without modification or rescission.

IN WITNESS WHEREOF, I have executed my name as Secretary and have hereunto affixed the corporate seal of the above-named Corporation this   day of   ,
        (year).

A True Record.

Attest.

_____
Secretary

RESOLUTION:
APPROVE FINANCIAL COUNSELING PLAN

WHEREAS, the Board of Directors of this Corporation deems it advisable to provide employees professional financial counseling at a cost to be entirely borne by the Corporation; be it

RESOLVED, that the Corporation adopt a Financial Counseling Plan for its employees on those specifications as have been presented to this Board and are annexed hereto; and

RESOLVED FURTHER, that the President and/or Treasurer of this Corporation is directed to undertake all actions as are necessary to implement and administer said plan.

The undersigned hereby certifies that he/she is the duly elected and qualified Secretary and the custodian of the books and records and seal of ,
a corporation duly formed pursuant to the laws of the State of ,
and that the foregoing is a true record of a resolution duly adopted at a meeting of the Board of Directors, and that said meeting was held in accordance with state law and the Bylaws of the above-named Corporation on , (year), and that said resolution is now in full force and effect without modification or rescission.

IN WITNESS WHEREOF, I have executed my name as Secretary and have hereunto affixed the corporate seal of the above-named Corporation this   day of ,
(year).

A True Record.

Attest.

_____
Secretary

RESOLUTION:
APPROVE GROUP LEGAL BENEFITS

WHEREAS, the Board of Directors of this Corporation deems it advisable to institute a group legal services plan for purposes of providing low-cost or no-cost legal services to employees and members of their families; be it

RESOLVED, that the Corporation adopt a Group Legal Services Plan in accordance with the specifications for a Group Legal Services Plan as presented to this Board and annexed hereto; and

RESOLVED FURTHER, that the President and/or Treasurer of the Corporation undertake all actions as are necessary to implement and administer said program.

The undersigned hereby certifies that he/she is the duly elected and qualified Secretary and the custodian of the books and records and seal of   , a corporation duly formed pursuant to the laws of the State of   , and that the foregoing is a true record of a resolution duly adopted at a meeting of the Board of Directors, and that said meeting was held in accordance with state law and the Bylaws of the above-named Corporation on   ,   (year), and that said resolution is now in full force and effect without modification or rescission.

IN WITNESS WHEREOF, I have executed my name as Secretary and have hereunto affixed the corporate seal of the above-named Corporation this   day of   , (year).

A True Record.

Attest.

_____
Secretary

RESOLUTION:
APPROVE HONORARIUM

WHEREAS, valuable services have been rendered to this Corporation by

, and

WHEREAS, the Board wishes to recognize said services and reward same by payment of a special honorarium; be it

RESOLVED, that the Corporation pay an honorarium of $ to

, in recognition of the special services granted the Corporation, and that the directors of the Corporation be directed to pay same forthwith.

The undersigned hereby certifies that he/she is the duly elected and qualified Secretary and the custodian of the books and records and seal of   ,
a corporation duly formed pursuant to the laws of the State of   ,
and that the foregoing is a true record of a resolution duly adopted at a meeting of the Board of Directors, and that said meeting was held in accordance with state law and the Bylaws of the above-named Corporation on   ,   (year), and that said resolution is now in full force and effect without modification or rescission.

IN WITNESS WHEREOF, I have executed my name as Secretary and have hereunto affixed the corporate seal of the above-named Corporation this   day of   ,

(year).

A True Record.

Attest.

_____
Secretary

RESOLUTION:
APPROVE LIFE INSURANCE BENEFITS

WHEREAS, it is the decision of the Board of Directors that the availability of a group life program is in the best interests of the Corporation as it will encourage improved employee relations and aid in the recruitment and retention of valuable employees and serve generally as a benefit to employees, be it

RESOLVED, that the Corporation purchase and acquire group insurance for those employees entitled to participate in said benefit in that said employee has been employed by the Corporation for at least   years, that the amount of insurance coverage be $ per employee, and that the entire cost of said insurance be borne by the Corporation. It is

RESOLVED FURTHER, that the President of the Corporation obtain said insurance from such insurance firm or firms which in the President's judgment is most satisfactory.

The undersigned hereby certifies that he/she is the duly elected and qualified Secretary and the custodian of the books and records and seal of   , a corporation duly formed pursuant to the laws of the State of   , and that the foregoing is a true record of a resolution duly adopted at a meeting of the Board of Directors, and that said meeting was held in accordance with state law and the Bylaws of the above-named Corporation on   ,   (year), and that said resolution is now in full force and effect without modification or rescission.

IN WITNESS WHEREOF, I have executed my name as Secretary and have hereunto affixed the corporate seal of the above-named Corporation this   day of   ,

(year).

A True Record.

Attest.

_____
Secretary

RESOLUTION:
APPROVE OFFICER BONUSES

WHEREAS, the Board is desirous of making certain cash bonuses to the various officers of the Corporation, all in recognition of their devoted service to the Corporation over this year; be it

RESOLVED, that the officers of the Corporation receive the bonuses as follows:

To_____ Chairman, $_____

To_____ President, $_____

To_____ Vice President, $_____

To_____ Treasurer, $_____

To_____ Secretary, $_____

RESOLVED FURTHER, that the Treasurer of the Corporation is directed to issue the above cash bonuses in accordance with the above specifications.

The undersigned hereby certifies that he/she is the duly elected and qualified Secretary and the custodian of the books and records and seal of _____ , a corporation duly formed pursuant to the laws of the State of _____ , and that the foregoing is a true record of a resolution duly adopted at a meeting of the Board of Directors, and that said meeting was held in accordance with state law and the Bylaws of the above-named Corporation on _____ , _____ (year), and that said resolution is now in full force and effect without modification or rescission.

IN WITNESS WHEREOF, I have executed my name as Secretary and have hereunto affixed the corporate seal of the above-named Corporation this _____ day of _____ , _____ (year).

A True Record.

Attest.

_____
Secretary

RESOLUTION:
APPROVE PENSION PLAN

WHEREAS, the Board of Directors of this Corporation deems it advisable to provide for the financial and retirement security of its employees; be it

RESOLVED, that the Corporation adopt a Pension Plan in accordance with the provisions and specifications as have been presented to and reviewed by this Board, and as said specifications are further annexed hereto; and, be it

RESOLVED FURTHER, that the President and/or Treasurer of the Corporation be directed to undertake such acts as are necessary to implement and administer said plan.

The undersigned hereby certifies that he/she is the duly elected and qualified Secretary and the custodian of the books and records and seal of   ,
a corporation duly formed pursuant to the laws of the State of   ,
and that the foregoing is a true record of a resolution duly adopted at a meeting of the Board of Directors, and that said meeting was held in accordance with state law and the Bylaws of the above-named Corporation on   ,   (year), and that said resolution is now in full force and effect without modification or rescission.

IN WITNESS WHEREOF, I have executed my name as Secretary and have hereunto affixed the corporate seal of the above-named Corporation this   day of   ,
        (year).

A True Record.

Attest.

_____
Secretary

RESOLUTION:
APPROVE PROFIT-SHARING PLAN

WHEREAS, the Board of Directors of this Corporation considers it to be in the best interests of the Corporation to adopt an employee Profit-Sharing Plan as a means of improving employee incentive and performance; be it

RESOLVED, that the Corporation adopt an employee Profit-Sharing Plan as presented to the Board, the specifications of which are annexed hereto, provided however that adoption shall be conditional upon (1) duly voted shareholder approval, and (2) a favorable ruling from the IRS that the plan, as constituted, qualifies under Sections 401 (a) and 404 of the Internal Revenue Code of 1954, as amended, and

RESOLVED FURTHER, that upon satisfaction of the conditions stated, the President and/or Treasurer undertake all actions as are necessary to implement and administer the plan.

The undersigned hereby certifies that he/she is the duly elected and qualified Secretary and the custodian of the books and records and seal of   ,
a corporation duly formed pursuant to the laws of the State of   ,
and that the foregoing is a true record of a resolution duly adopted at a meeting of the Board of Directors, and that said meeting was held in accordance with state law and the Bylaws of the above-named Corporation on   ,   (year), and that said resolution is now in full force and effect without modification or rescission.

IN WITNESS WHEREOF, I have executed my name as Secretary and have hereunto affixed the corporate seal of the above-named Corporation this   day of   ,
        (year).

A True Record.

Attest.

_____
Secretary

RESOLUTION:
APPROVE QUALIFIED STOCK OPTION PLAN

WHEREAS, the Board of Directors of this Corporation has determined that certain officers and key employees should have available to them an option to buy shares of the Corporation under a qualified Stock Option Plan; be it

RESOLVED, that the Corporation adopt a Stock Option Plan in accordance with the provisions and specifications of the Stock Option Plan presented to and reviewed by the Board, a copy of said specifications being annexed hereto; and, be it

RESOLVED FURTHER, that the Corporation shall set aside a total of

(   ) shares of the common stock of the Corporation for sale to officers and key employees under the plan, and all as further approved by the shareholders; and, be it

RESOLVED FURTHER, that the President and/or Treasurer of the Corporation shall undertake all actions necessary to implement and administer said plan.

The undersigned hereby certifies that he/she is the duly elected and qualified Secretary and the custodian of the books and records and seal of   ,

a corporation duly formed pursuant to the laws of the State of   ,

and that the foregoing is a true record of a resolution duly adopted at a meeting of the Board of Directors, and that said meeting was held in accordance with state law and the Bylaws of the above-named Corporation on   ,   (year), and that said resolution is now in full force and effect without modification or rescission.

IN WITNESS WHEREOF, I have executed my name as Secretary and have hereunto affixed the corporate seal of the above-named Corporation this   day of   ,

(year).

A True Record.

Attest.

_____
Secretary

RESOLUTION:
APPROVE SPLIT-DOLLAR INSURANCE

WHEREAS, it is the decision of the Board of Directors that a Split-Dollar Insurance Program be instituted as a fringe benefit and to make available adequate insurance to protect their families in the event of death; be it

RESOLVED, that the Corporation negotiate the purchase of Split-Dollar Life Insurance and adopt a Split-Dollar Insurance Benefit Program, all in accordance with the specifications for said insurance program as presented to the Board and annexed hereto. And, it is

RESOLVED FURTHER, that the President of the Corporation be authorized to negotiate and purchase such insurance from such underwriters, and on such terms as the president deems to be in the best interests of the Corporation.

The undersigned hereby certifies that he/she is the duly elected and qualified Secretary and the custodian of the books and records and seal of   ,

a corporation duly formed pursuant to the laws of the State of   ,

and that the foregoing is a true record of a resolution duly adopted at a meeting of the Board of Directors, and that said meeting was held in accordance with state law and the Bylaws of the above-named Corporation on   ,   (year), and that said resolution is now in full force and effect without modification or rescission.

IN WITNESS WHEREOF, I have executed my name as Secretary and have hereunto affixed the corporate seal of the above-named Corporation this   day of   ,

(year).

A True Record.

Attest.

_____
Secretary

FORM R720

RESOLUTION:
APPROVE STOCK BONUS TO DIRECTORS

WHEREAS, the Board of Directors is desirous of making certain bonuses available to the officers of the Corporation in the form of shares of common stock; be it

RESOLVED, that the following officers of the Corporation be issued as a bonus the number of shares of common stock of the Corporation as is set forth opposite their respective names:

Name	Title	Number of Shares
_____	_____	_____
_____	_____	_____
_____	_____	_____
_____	_____	_____
_____	_____	_____

The undersigned hereby certifies that he/she is the duly elected and qualified Secretary and the custodian of the books and records and seal of   ,
a corporation duly formed pursuant to the laws of the State of   ,
and that the foregoing is a true record of a resolution duly adopted at a meeting of the Board of Directors, and that said meeting was held in accordance with state law and the Bylaws of the above-named Corporation on   ,   (year), and that said resolution is now in full force and effect without modification or rescission.

IN WITNESS WHEREOF, I have executed my name as Secretary and have hereunto affixed the corporate seal of the above-named Corporation this   day of   ,
        (year).

A True Record.

Attest.

_____
Secretary

RESOLUTION:
APPROVE STOCK OPTION PLAN

RESOLVED, that the Stock Option Plan attached to this resolution is hereby approved, and

RESOLVED FURTHER, that the Board of Directors is hereby authorized to set aside a total of   (   ) shares of the common stock without par value of this Corporation, pursuant to the increase in the capital stock duly authorized by the stockholders of this Corporation on   ,
(year), for sale and issuance to the executives and key employees of this Corporation upon the terms of said Stock Option Plan.

The undersigned hereby certifies that he/she is the duly elected and qualified Secretary and the custodian of the books and records and seal of   ,
a corporation duly formed pursuant to the laws of the State of   ,
and that the foregoing is a true record of a resolution duly adopted at a meeting of the Board of Directors, and that said meeting was held in accordance with state law and the Bylaws of the above-named Corporation on   ,   (year), and that said resolution is now in full force and effect without modification or rescission.

IN WITNESS WHEREOF, I have executed my name as Secretary and have hereunto affixed the corporate seal of the above-named Corporation this   day of   ,
        (year).

A True Record.

Attest.

_____
Secretary

RESOLUTION:
AUTHORIZE BONUS BASED ON PROFITS

RESOLVED, that there shall be paid as special compensation for the services rendered

by   as   of this

Corporation, at   percent (%) of the net profits of this Corporation

during the year   , as evidenced by the books of the Corporation, but shall not exceed

the sum of

Dollars ($), the said special compensation to be paid to

at the end of the fiscal year   , and

RESOLVED FURTHER, that for the purpose of fixing such compensation, net profits

shall mean the amount available on net income after deductions for interest on

indebtedness, expenses, all accrued taxes, and preferred dividends.

The undersigned hereby certifies that he/she is the duly elected and qualified Secretary

and the custodian of the books and records and seal of   ,

a corporation duly formed pursuant to the laws of the State of   ,

and that the foregoing is a true record of a resolution duly adopted at a meeting of the

Board of Directors, and that said meeting was held in accordance with state law and the

Bylaws of the above-named Corporation on   ,   (year), and that

said resolution is now in full force and effect without modification or rescission.

IN WITNESS WHEREOF, I have executed my name as Secretary and have hereunto

affixed the corporate seal of the above-named Corporation this   day of   ,

(year).

A True Record.

Attest.

_____
Secretary

RESOLUTION:
AUTHORIZE CHARGE ACCOUNT

RESOLVED, that   as   of

the Corporation is hereby authorized to establish a credit account with

, and to charge to said account any travel, entertainment and

other expenses related to the ordinary and necessary trade or business of this Corporation,

which expenses the Treasurer is hereby authorized and directed to pay as they become

due.

The undersigned hereby certifies that he/she is the duly elected and qualified Secretary

and the custodian of the books and records and seal of   ,

a corporation duly formed pursuant to the laws of the State of   ,

and that the foregoing is a true record of a resolution duly adopted at a meeting of the

Board of Directors, and that said meeting was held in accordance with state law and the

Bylaws of the above-named Corporation on   ,   (year), and that

said resolution is now in full force and effect without modification or rescission.

IN WITNESS WHEREOF, I have executed my name as Secretary and have hereunto

affixed the corporate seal of the above-named Corporation this   day of   ,

(year).

A True Record.

Attest.

_____
Secretary

RESOLUTION:
AUTHORIZE CHRISTMAS BONUS

WHEREAS, it is in the best interests of the Corporation to motivate its employees with a Christmas bonus; be it

RESOLVED, that the Corporation allocate the sum of

Dollars ($) for Christmas bonuses, and

FURTHER RESOLVED, that bonuses be paid to each employee in accordance with the Christmas Bonus Schedule as annexed hereto.

The undersigned hereby certifies that he/she is the duly elected and qualified Secretary and the custodian of the books and records and seal of   ,
a corporation duly formed pursuant to the laws of the State of   ,
and that the foregoing is a true record of a resolution duly adopted at a meeting of the Board of Directors, and that said meeting was held in accordance with state law and the Bylaws of the above-named Corporation on   ,   (year), and that said resolution is now in full force and effect without modification or rescission.

IN WITNESS WHEREOF, I have executed my name as Secretary and have hereunto affixed the corporate seal of the above-named Corporation this   day of   ,
(year).

A True Record.

Attest.

_____
Secretary

RESOLUTION:
AUTHORIZE COUNTRY CLUB MEMBERSHIP

WHEREAS, the Board of Directors has determined that a Country Club membership would enhance the ability of the Corporation to entertain business clients and thereupon conduct more business; be it

RESOLVED, that the Corporation apply for membership at the

Country Club, either in its own name or in the name of

as   of the Corporation; and that the Corporation pay all costs associated with membership or related to the entertainment of business clients.

The undersigned hereby certifies that he/she is the duly elected and qualified Secretary and the custodian of the books and records and seal of   ,
a corporation duly formed pursuant to the laws of the State of   ,
and that the foregoing is a true record of a resolution duly adopted at a meeting of the Board of Directors, and that said meeting was held in accordance with state law and the Bylaws of the above-named Corporation on   ,   (year), and that said resolution is now in full force and effect without modification or rescission.

IN WITNESS WHEREOF, I have executed my name as Secretary and have hereunto affixed the corporate seal of the above-named Corporation this   day of   ,

        (year).

A True Record.

Attest.

_____
Secretary

RESOLUTION:
AUTHORIZE DIRECTORS' COMPENSATION

WHEREAS, it is in the best interests of the Corporation to provide compensation to directors upon their attendance at meetings; be it

RESOLVED, that the Corporation pay to each director attending any regular or special meeting of the board the sum of $ per meeting, inclusive of any adjournment thereof, and that said compensation policy commence with the next held meeting of the board.

The undersigned hereby certifies that he/she is the duly elected and qualified Secretary and the custodian of the books and records and seal of   ,
a corporation duly formed pursuant to the laws of the State of   ,
and that the foregoing is a true record of a resolution duly adopted at a meeting of the Board of Directors, and that said meeting was held in accordance with state law and the Bylaws of the above-named Corporation on   ,   (year), and that said resolution is now in full force and effect without modification or rescission.

IN WITNESS WHEREOF, I have executed my name as Secretary and have hereunto affixed the corporate seal of the above-named Corporation this   day of   ,
        (year).

A True Record.

Attest.

_____
Secretary

RESOLUTION:
AUTHORIZE GROUP MEDICAL/DENTAL BENEFITS

WHEREAS, the Board of Directors has determined that it is in the best interests of the Corporation to offer its employees a Group Medical/Dental Plan; be it

RESOLVED, that the Corporation adopt the Group Medical/Dental Plan as presented to and reviewed by the board and is further annexed hereto, and

RESOLVED FURTHER, that the President and/or Treasurer of the Corporation undertake all actions as are necessary to administer and implement said plan.

The undersigned hereby certifies that he/she is the duly elected and qualified Secretary and the custodian of the books and records and seal of   , a corporation duly formed pursuant to the laws of the State of   , and that the foregoing is a true record of a resolution duly adopted at a meeting of the Board of Directors, and that said meeting was held in accordance with state law and the Bylaws of the above-named Corporation on   ,   (year), and that said resolution is now in full force and effect without modification or rescission.

IN WITNESS WHEREOF, I have executed my name as Secretary and have hereunto affixed the corporate seal of the above-named Corporation this   day of   ,
        (year).

A True Record.

Attest.

_____
Secretary

RESOLUTION:
AUTHORIZE LEAVE OF ABSENCE

WHEREAS,   has been employed by the

Corporation since   and now requests a personal leave of absence; be

it

RESOLVED, that   is hereby granted a leave of

absence from the Corporation for the period from   ,   (year), to

            ,   (year). Compensation and continuity of fringe benefits during

this absence shall be as provided in the annexed letter authorizing said leave.

The undersigned hereby certifies that he/she is the duly elected and qualified Secretary

and the custodian of the books and records and seal of   ,

a corporation duly formed pursuant to the laws of the State of   ,

and that the foregoing is a true record of a resolution duly adopted at a meeting of the

Board of Directors, and that said meeting was held in accordance with state law and the

Bylaws of the above-named Corporation on   ,   (year), and that

said resolution is now in full force and effect without modification or rescission.

IN WITNESS WHEREOF, I have executed my name as Secretary and have hereunto

affixed the corporate seal of the above-named Corporation this   day of   ,

        (year).

A True Record.

Attest.

_____

Secretary

RESOLUTION:
AUTHORIZE RAISE

WHEREAS,   as   of

the Corporation currently earns $ per year as a salary, and

WHEREAS, the Corporation wishes to recognize said individual's performance and

contributions to the Corporation by granting a raise; be it

RESOLVED, that the present salary of $ per annum be raised to $

per annum, effective as of   ,   (year).

The undersigned hereby certifies that he/she is the duly elected and qualified Secretary

and the custodian of the books and records and seal of   ,

a corporation duly formed pursuant to the laws of the State of   ,

and that the foregoing is a true record of a resolution duly adopted at a meeting of the

Board of Directors, and that said meeting was held in accordance with state law and the

Bylaws of the above-named Corporation on   ,   (year), and that

said resolution is now in full force and effect without modification or rescission.

IN WITNESS WHEREOF, I have executed my name as Secretary and have hereunto

affixed the corporate seal of the above-named Corporation this   day of   ,

        (year).

A True Record.

Attest.

_____
                                                Secretary

RESOLUTION:
FIX SALARY

RESOLVED, that the salary of the   of the Corporation be fixed at

$ per annum, until further action by the board.

The undersigned hereby certifies that he/she is the duly elected and qualified Secretary

and the custodian of the books and records and seal of   ,

a corporation duly formed pursuant to the laws of the State of   ,

and that the foregoing is a true record of a resolution duly adopted at a meeting of the

Board of Directors, and that said meeting was held in accordance with state law and the

Bylaws of the above-named Corporation on   ,   (year), and that

said resolution is now in full force and effect without modification or rescission.

IN WITNESS WHEREOF, I have executed my name as Secretary and have hereunto

affixed the corporate seal of the above-named Corporation this   day of   ,

(year).

A True Record.

Attest.

_____
Secretary

RESOLUTION:
MAKE CHARITABLE CONTRIBUTION

WHEREAS, the Board of Directors deems it to be in the best interests of the Corporation to make a charitable contribution to

; be it

RESOLVED, that the Corporation donate to

the generally described assets of the Corporation as:

; and be it

RESOLVED FURTHER, that the President and/or Treasurer obtain from counsel an opinion that said contribution qualifies as a(n)   expense pursuant to Internal Revenue Service regulations.

The undersigned hereby certifies that he/she is the duly elected and qualified Secretary and the custodian of the books and records and seal of   ,

a corporation duly formed pursuant to the laws of the State of   ,

and that the foregoing is a true record of a resolution duly adopted at a meeting of the Board of Directors, and that said meeting was held in accordance with state law and the Bylaws of the above-named Corporation on   ,   (year), and that said resolution is now in full force and effect without modification or rescission.

IN WITNESS WHEREOF, I have executed my name as Secretary and have hereunto affixed the corporate seal of the above-named Corporation this   day of   ,

(year).

A True Record.

Attest.

_____
Secretary

RESOLUTION:
MODIFY OFFICER SALARIES

RESOLVED, that the salaries of the officers of the Corporation be adjusted as follows, effective immediately:

President from $_____   to $_____

Vice President from $_____   to $_____

Treasurer from $_____   to $_____

Secretary from $_____   to $_____

And that said salaries remain in force until further action by this board.

The undersigned hereby certifies that he/she is the duly elected and qualified Secretary and the custodian of the books and records and seal of   , a corporation duly formed pursuant to the laws of the State of   , and that the foregoing is a true record of a resolution duly adopted at a meeting of the Board of Directors, and that said meeting was held in accordance with state law and the Bylaws of the above-named Corporation on   ,   (year), and that said resolution is now in full force and effect without modification or rescission.

IN WITNESS WHEREOF, I have executed my name as Secretary and have hereunto affixed the corporate seal of the above-named Corporation this   day of   ,
(year).

A True Record.

Attest.

_____
Secretary

RESOLUTION:
PAY OFFICER BONUSES

WHEREAS,   presented to this board
recommendations for bonuses to officers, as follows:

To _____, President, $ _____

To _____, Vice President, $ _____

To _____, Secretary, $ _____

To _____, Treasurer, $ _____

RESOLVED, that the said recommendations are hereby approved and adopted, and that the Treasurer of this Corporation is hereby authorized and directed to make payments to the respective officers, in accordance with the above recommendations.

The undersigned hereby certifies that he/she is the duly elected and qualified Secretary and the custodian of the books and records and seal of   ,
a corporation duly formed pursuant to the laws of the State of   ,
and that the foregoing is a true record of a resolution duly adopted at a meeting of the Board of Directors, and that said meeting was held in accordance with state law and the Bylaws of the above-named Corporation on   ,   (year), and that said resolution is now in full force and effect without modification or rescission.

IN WITNESS WHEREOF, I have executed my name as Secretary and have hereunto affixed the corporate seal of the above-named Corporation this   day of   ,
(year).

A True Record.

Attest.

_____
Secretary

RESOLUTION:
REPAY EXCESS COMPENSATION

RESOLVED, that each officer of the Corporation shall be responsible to repay to the Corporation any amount paid to such officer as salary that has been disallowed by the Internal Revenue Service as excess salary or compensation.

The undersigned hereby certifies that he/she is the duly elected and qualified Secretary and the custodian of the books and records and seal of   ,
a corporation duly formed pursuant to the laws of the State of   ,
and that the foregoing is a true record of a resolution duly adopted at a meeting of the Board of Directors, and that said meeting was held in accordance with state law and the Bylaws of the above-named Corporation on   ,   (year), and that said resolution is now in full force and effect without modification or rescission.

IN WITNESS WHEREOF, I have executed my name as Secretary and have hereunto affixed the corporate seal of the above-named Corporation this   day of   ,
            (year).

A True Record.

Attest.

_____
Secretary

RESOLUTION:
STOCK BONUS FOR OFFICERS

RESOLVED, that as additional compensation and bonus for their services to

_____ , _____ (year), there shall be issued to the following

officers of the company the number of shares of common stock of this Corporation as set

opposite their respective names:

Officer	Position	Number of Shares
_____	_____	_____
_____	_____	_____
_____	_____	_____
_____	_____	_____

The undersigned hereby certifies that he/she is the duly elected and qualified Secretary

and the custodian of the books and records and seal of _____ ,

a corporation duly formed pursuant to the laws of the State of _____ ,

and that the foregoing is a true record of a resolution duly adopted at a meeting of the

Board of Directors, and that said meeting was held in accordance with state law and the

Bylaws of the above-named Corporation on _____ , _____ (year), and that

said resolution is now in full force and effect without modification or rescission.

IN WITNESS WHEREOF, I have executed my name as Secretary and have hereunto

affixed the corporate seal of the above-named Corporation this _____ day of _____ ,

_____ (year).

A True Record.

Attest.

_____
Secretary

RESOLUTION:
TERMINATE OFFICER SALARIES

RESOLVED, that the salaries of the President, Vice President, Secretary and Treasurer of this Corporation, as fixed by resolution of the Board of Directors at a meeting held on _____ , _____ (year), shall be terminated as of _____ , _____ (year); that the said officers shall serve the Corporation as such officers without compensation; and that no salaries shall be paid to the said officers until authorized by the Board of Directors.

The undersigned hereby certifies that he/she is the duly elected and qualified Secretary and the custodian of the books and records and seal of _____ , a corporation duly formed pursuant to the laws of the State of _____ , and that the foregoing is a true record of a resolution duly adopted at a meeting of the Board of Directors, and that said meeting was held in accordance with state law and the Bylaws of the above-named Corporation on _____ , _____ (year), and that said resolution is now in full force and effect without modification or rescission.

IN WITNESS WHEREOF, I have executed my name as Secretary and have hereunto affixed the corporate seal of the above-named Corporation this _____ day of _____ , _____ (year).

A True Record.

Attest.

_____
Secretary

Glossary of useful terms

A-C

Assets

Anything owned with monetary value. This includes both real and personal property.

Authorized shares

The number of shares a corporation is authorized to sell.

Bylaws

Rules adopted by the corporation itself for the regulation of a corporation's own actions; a subordinate law adopted by a corporation, association, or other body for its self-government or to regulate the rights and duties of its officers and members.

C corporation

A regular corporation that is not an S corporation.

Calendar year

The accounting year beginning on January 1 and ending on December 31.

Certificate or Articles of Incorporation

The document that creates a corporation according to the laws of the state. This must be filed and approved by the state.

C-I

Consolidation

When two corporations combine, creating a third.

Deceptively similar

A name so similar to another name that the two become confused in the public eye.

Dividend income

Dividends that must be declared as regular income for income tax purposes.

Fiscal year

Any 12-month period used by a business as its fiscal accounting period. Such accounting period may, for example, run from July 1 of one year through June 30 of the next year.

Foreign corporation

A corporation formed in one state or country but conducting some or all of its business in another state or country.

Incorporate

To form a corporation or to organize and be granted status as a corporation by following procedures prescribed by law.

Incorporator

The person who signs the Articles of Incorporation upon petitioning the state for a corporate charter.

Insolvency

Being unable to pay one's debts; bankruptcy because liabilities exceed assets.

Issued shares

The number of shares actually sold by the corporation.

M-P

Merger

The absorption of one corporation by another.

Minority stockholder

One who owns or controls less than 50 percent of the stock in a corporation.

Minutes

Written records of formal proceedings of stockholders' and directors' meetings.

Non-par value stock

Shares of stock without specified value.

Not-for-profit corporation

A corporation organized for some charitable, civil, social or other purpose that does not entail the generation of profit or the distribution of its income to members, principals, shareholders, officers or others affiliated with it. Such corporations are accorded special treatment under the law for some purposes, including taxation.

Parliamentary procedure

Rules such as "Roberts Rules of Order," which govern stockholders' meetings, directors' meetings, etc.

Par value stock

Shares of stock with a specified value.

Proxy

Authorization by a stockholder allowing another to vote his shares of stock.

P-St

Publicly owned corporation

One whose stock is owned by more than 25 stockholders and is regulated by the Securities and Exchange Commission.

Quorum

A majority of the stockholders or directors necessary for vote-counting and decision-making at a meeting. While a quorum is usually a majority of either the total membership or the members present, a quorum may consist of a greater number than a simple majority if desired and stated in the bylaws.

Regular corporation

Also known as a C Corporation.

S Corporation (Subchapter S Corporation)

A small business corporation which elects to be taxed as a partnership or proprietorship for federal income tax purposes. Individual shareholders enjoy the benefits under state law of limited corporate liability, but avoid corporate federal taxes.

Service business

A business that sells service or advice instead of a tangible product..

Shareholder

See Stockholder.

Start-up venture

A new business having no track record.

State statutes

Laws created by a state legislature.

St-Su

Statutory agent

A lawyer, corporation or individual who has assumed the responsibility of being the legal representative for the corporation for purposes of accepting legal service in a certain state.

Stock certificate

Written instrument evidencing a share in the ownership of a corporation.

Stockholder

A holder of one or more shares of the stock of a corporation. A stockholder may be called a "shareholder."

Subsidiary

A corporation owned by another corporation.

Resources

Where you'll find these Resources:

••• Departments of Incorporation •••

ALABAMA
Secretary of State
State Capitol Corporations Div.
P.O. Box 5616
Montgomery, AL 36103-5616
(334) 242-5324

ALASKA
State of Alaska
Department of Commerce and
Economic Development
Div. of Banking, Securities &
Corporations
Juneau, AL 99811-0807
(907) 465-2521

ARIZONA
Arizona Corporation Commission
Incorporating Division
1300 W. Washington St., 3rd Floor
Phoenix, AZ 85007
(602) 542-4786

ARKANSAS
Secretary of State–Corporations Div.
Aegon Building
501 Woodlane, Suite 310
Little Rock, AR 72201-1094
(501) 682-3409

CALIFORNIA
Secretary of State
1500 11th Street, 6th Floor
Sacramento, CA 95814
(916) 653-6814

COLORADO
Secretary of State
1560 Broadway, Suite 200
Denver, CO 80202
(303) 894-2200

CONNECTICUT
Office of the Secretary of State
State of Connecticut
Corporations Division
30 Trinity Street
Hartford, CT 06106
(860) 509-6000

DELAWARE
State of Delaware
Division of Corporations
P.O. Box 898
Dover, DE 19903
(302) 739-3073

DISTRICT OF COLUMBIA
Dept. of Consumer Reg. Affairs
614 "H" Street N.W., Rm 407
Washington, DC 20001
(202) 727-7278

FLORIDA
Division of Corporations
P.O. Box 6327
Tallahassee, FL 32314
(850) 488-9000

GEORGIA
Secretary of State
Corporations Department
2 Martin Luther King Junior Drive
Suite 315, West Tower
Atlanta, GA 30334
(404) 656-2817

HAWAII
Dept. of Commerce & Consumer Affairs
Business Registration Division
P.O. Box 40
Honolulu, HI 96810
(808) 586-2744

IDAHO
Secretary of State
P.O. Box 83720
Boise, ID 83720-0080
(208) 334-2300

ILLINOIS
Secretary of State
Department of Corporations
328 Howlett Building-Business Services
Springfield, IL 62756
(217) 782-7880

INDIANA
Secretary of State-Corporation Division
302 W. Washington St., Rm E018
Indianapolis, IN 46204
(317) 232-6576

IOWA
Secretary of State-Corporation Division
Hoover Blvd. 2nd Floor
Des Moines, IA 50319
(515) 281-7563

KANSAS
Secretary of State
Statehouse, 2nd Floor
300 SW 10th Street
Topeka, KS 66612-1594
(913) 296-4564

KENTUCKY
Secretary of State–Corporations Div.
152 Capitol Building
700 Capitol Avenue
Frankfort, KY 40601
(502) 564-2848

LOUISIANA
Secretary of State–Corporations Div.
P.O. Box 94125
Baton Rouge, LA 70804-9125
(504) 925-4716

MAINE
Secretary of State
Department of Incorporation
101 State House Station
Augusta, ME 04333-0101
(207) 287-6308

MARYLAND
State Dept. of Assess. and Tax.
301 W. Preston St., Room 809
Baltimore, MD 21201-2395
(410) 767-1340

MASSACHUSETTS
Secretary of State
Corporations Division
State House Room 337
Boston, MA 02133
(617) 727-2853

MICHIGAN
State of Michigan
Dept of Commerce, Corp. Div.
6546 Mercantile Way
Lansing, MI 48911
(517) 334-7561

MINNESOTA
Secretary of State
100 Constitution Avenue, Rm 180
St. Paul, MN 55155-1299
(612) 215-1441

MISSISSIPPI
Secretary of State
Office of Incorporation
P.O. Box 136
Jackson, MS 39205
(601) 359-1350

MISSOURI
Secretary of State–Corporations Div.
P.O. Box 778
Jefferson City, MO 65102
(573) 751-1301

MONTANA
Secretary of State
P.O. Box 202801
Helena, MT 59620-2801
(406) 444-2034

NEBRASKA
Secretary of State
Corporate Division
P.O. Box 94608
Lincoln, NB 68509
(402) 471-4079

NEVADA
Secretary of State
101 N. Carson Street
Carson City, NV 89701
(702) 687-5203

NEW HAMPSHIRE
Secretary of State–Corporations Div.
State House
107 Main Street, Room 204
Concord, NH 03301-4989
(603) 271-3246

NEW JERSEY
Secretary of State
P.O. Box 300
Trenton, NJ 08625
(609) 530-6431

NEW MEXICO
State Corporation Commission
P.O. Box 1269
Santa Fe, NM 87504-1269
(505) 827-4500

NEW YORK
Secretary of State–Corporations Div.
41 State Street
Albany, NY 12231
(518) 474-6200

NORTH CAROLINA
Secretary of State–Corporations Div.
300 North Salisbury Street
Raleigh, NC 27603-5909
(919) 733-4161

NORTH DAKOTA
Secretary of State–Corporations Div.
600 East Boulevard Avenue
Bismark, ND 58505
(701) 328-4284

OHIO
Secretary of State
30 East Broad Street, 14th Floor
Columbus, OH 43266-0418
(614) 466-1145

OKLAHOMA
Secretary of State
2300 N. Lincoln, Room 101
Oklahoma City, OK 73105
(405) 521-3911

OREGON
Secretary of State
Corporation Division
255 Capitol Street NE
Salem, OR 97310-1327
(503) 986-2200

PENNSYLVANIA
Commonwealth of Pennsylvania
Corporations Office
North Office Bldg., Room 302
Harrisburg, PA 17120
(717) 787-4057

PUERTO RICO
Commonwealth of Puerto Rico
Department of State
PO Box 9023271
San Juan, PR 00902-3271
(787) 722-2121

RHODE ISLAND
Secretary of State
Corporations Office
State House, Room 220
Providence, RI 02903
(401) 277-3040

SOUTH CAROLINA
Secretary of State
P.O. Box 11350
Columbia, SC 29211
(803) 734-2158

SOUTH DAKOTA
Secretary of State
Attn: Corporations
500 E. Capitol, Suite 204
Pierre, SD 57501
(605) 773-4845

TENNESSEE
Secretary of State–Corporations Div.
State Capitol, 1st Floor
Nashville, TN 37243-0305
(615) 741-0529

TEXAS
Secretary of State–Corporations Div.
P.O. Box 13697
Austin, TX 78711-3697
(512) 463-5586

UTAH
Department of Commerce
P.O. Box 146791
Salt Lake City, UT 84114-6701
(801) 530-6027

VERMONT
Secretary of State
Corporations Division
109 State Street
Montpelier, VT 05609-1101
(802) 828-2386

VIRGINIA
Commonwealth of Virginia
State Corporation Commission
P.O. Box 1197
Richmond, VA 23218
(804) 371-9376

WASHINGTON
Secretary of State
Corporation Division
P.O. Box 40220
Olympia, WA 98504-0220
(360) 753-2896

WEST VIRGINIA
Secretary of State–Corporations Div.
1900 Kanawha Boulevard E
Building 1, Suite 157-K
Charleston, WV 25305-0770
(304) 558-8000

WISCONSIN
Department of Financial Institutions
Corporations and Consumer Division
P.O. Box 7846
Madison, WI 53707-7846
(608) 261-9550

WYOMING
Secretary of State
Corporations Division
State Capitol Bldg.
Cheyenne, WY 82002-0020
(307) 777-7314

··· Online Resources ···

◆ **American Arbitration Association**

    URL: *http://www.adr.org*

◆ **American Consumer Credit Counseling**

    URL: *http://www.consumercredit.com*

◆ **American Express Small Business Exchange**

    URL: *http://www.americanexpress.com/smallbusiness*

◆ **American Society of Corporate Secretaries**

    URL: *http://www.ascs.org*

◆ **BizProWeb**

    URL: *http://www.bizproweb.com*

◆ **Commercial Law League of America**

    URL: *http://www.clla.org*

◆ **Corporate Finance Network–Corporate Governance**

    URL: *http://www.corpfinet.com/EP_Corp_Gov.html*

◆ **Council of Better Business Bureaus, Inc.**

    URL: *http://www.bbb.org*

◆ **Education Index, Business Resources**

> *URL:*   *http://www.educationindex.com/bus*

◆ **Employmentlawcenteral**

> *URL:*   *http://www.employmentlawcenteral.com*

◆ **Entrepreneur's Help Page**

> *URL:*   *http://www.tannedfeet.com*

◆ **Federal Trade Commission-Consumer Protection**

> *URL:*   *http://www.ftc.gov/bcp/menu-credit.htm*

◆ **Garrett Publishing, Inc.**

> *URL:*   *http://www.garrettpub.com*

◆ **International Finance & Commodities Institute**

> *URL:*   *http://finance.wat.ch/IFCI*

◆ **Lawlounge**

> *URL:*   *http://lawlounge.com/topics/corporate/main.htm*

◆ **National Association of Corporate Directors**

> *URL:*   *http://www.nacdonline.org/seminar_entrepren.htm*

◆ **National Center for Employee Ownership**

    URL: *http://www.nceo.org/index.html*

◆ **National Employee Rights Institute, NERI**

    URL: *http://www.nerinet.org*

◆ **National Federation of Independent Business**

    URL: *http://www.nfibonline.com*

◆ **National Small Business Development Center Research Network**

    URL: *http://www.smallbiz.suny.edu*

◆ **Small Business Advisor**

    URL: *http://www.isquare.com*

◆ **Small Business Primer**

    URL: *http://www.ces.ncsu.edu/depts/fcs/business/*
                                                welcome.html

◆ **U.S. Department of Labor**

    URL: *http://dol.gov/dol/welcome.htm*

◆ **U.S. Small Business Administration**

    URL: *http://www.sbaonline.sba.gov/starting*

◆ **U.S. Business Advisor**

    URL: *http://www.business.gov*

◆ **Work Doctor, The**

    URL: *http://www.workdoctor.com*

◆ **Yahoo! Small Business Information**

    URL: *http://dir.yahoo.com/Business_and_Economy/*
                      Small_Business_Information

••• Related Sites •••

◆ **American Bankruptcy Institute, The**

    URL: *http://www.abiworld.org*

◆ **Bankruptcy Online**

    URL: *http://www.fedfil.com/bankruptcy/index.html*

◆ **Center for Debt Management**

    URL: *http://www.center4debtmanagement.com*

◆ **Debt Counselors of America**

    URL: *http://www.dca.org/home.htm*

◆ **e-Bankruptcy.com**

    URL: *http://www.e-bankruptcy.com*

◆ **Equifax, Inc.**

    URL: *http://www.equifax.com*

◆ **Experian Information Solutions, Inc.**

    URL: *http://www.experian.com*

◆ **Findlaw's bankruptcy site**

    URL: *http://www.findlaw.com/01topics/03bankruptcy*
                                     /index.html

◆ **Institute of Certified Financial Planners**

    URL: *http://www.icfp.org*

◆ **International Association for Financial Planning**

    URL: *http://www.iafp.org*

◆ **InterNet Bankruptcy Library (IBL)**

    URL: *http://bankrupt.com*

◆ **Links to Bankruptcy Related Sites**

    URL: *http://www.iimagers.com/bankruptcy.html*

◆ **National Association of Personal Financial Advisors**

    URL: *http://www.napfa.org*

◆ **National Foundation for Consumer Credit (NFCC), The**

    URL: *http://www.nfcc.org*

◆ **Pension and Welfare Benefits Administration**

    URL: *http://www.dol.gov/dol/pwba*

◆ **Trans Union LLC**

    URL: *http://www.transunion.com*

◆ **U.S. Equal Employment Opportunity Commission, The (EEOC)**

    URL: *http://www.eeoc.gov*

••• Legal Search Engines •••

◆ **All Law**

URL: *http://www.alllaw.com*

◆ **American Law Sources On Line**

URL: *http://www.lawsource.com/also/searchfm.htm*

◆ **Catalaw**

URL: *http://www.catalaw.com*

◆ **FindLaw**

URL: *http://www.findlaw.com*

◆ **Hieros Gamos**

URL: *http://www.hg.org/hg.html*

◆ **InternetOracle**

URL: *http://www.internetoracle.com/legal.htm*

◆ **LawAid**

URL: *http://www.lawaid.com/search.html*

◆ **LawCrawler**

URL: *http://www.lawcrawler.com*

◆ **LawEngine, The**

    URL: *http://www.fastsearch.com/law*

◆ **LawRunner**

    URL: *http://www.lawrunner.com*

◆ **'Lectric Law Library™**

    URL: *http://www.lectlaw.com*

◆ **Legal Search Engines**

    URL: *http://www.dreamscape.com/frankvad/search.legal.html*

◆ **LEXIS/NEXIS Communications Center**

    URL: *http://www.lexis-nexis.com/lncc/general/search.html*

◆ **Meta-Index for U.S. Legal Research**

    URL: *http://gsulaw.gsu.edu/metaindex*

◆ **Seamless Website, The**

    URL: *http://seamless.com*

◆ **USALaw**

    URL: *http://www.usalaw.com/linksrch.cfm*

◆ **WestLaw**

    URL: *http://westdoc.com* (Registered users only. Fee paid service.)

••• State Bar Associations •••

ALABAMA

Alabama State Bar
415 Dexter Avenue
Montgomery, AL 36104

mailing address:
PO Box 671
Montgomery, AL 36101
(205) 269-1515

http://www.alabar.org

ALASKA

Alaska Bar Association
510 L Street No. 602
Anchorage, AK 99501

mailing address
PO Box 100279
Anchorage, AK 99510

ARIZONA

State Bar of Arizona
111 West Monroe
Phoenix, AZ 85003-1742
(602) 252-4804

ARKANSAS

Arkansas Bar Association
400 West Markham
Little Rock, AR 72201
(501) 375-4605

CALIFORNIA

State Bar of California
555 Franklin Street
San Francisco, CA 94102
(415) 561-8200

http://www.calbar.org

Alameda County Bar
Association

http://www.acbanet.org

COLORADO

Colorado Bar Association
No. 950, 1900 Grant Street
Denver, CO 80203
(303) 860-1115

*http://www.usa.net/cobar/
index.htm*

CONNECTICUT

Connecticut Bar Association
101 Corporate Place
Rocky Hill, CT 06067-1894
(203) 721-0025

DELAWARE

Delaware State Bar Association
1225 King Street, 10th floor
Wilmington, DE 19801
(302) 658-5279
(302) 658-5278 (lawyer referral service)

DISTRICT OF COLUMBIA

District of Columbia Bar
1250 H Street, NW, 6th Floor
Washington, DC 20005
(202) 737-4700

Bar Association of the District of
Columbia
1819 H Street, NW, 12th floor
Washington, DC 20006-3690
(202) 223-6600

FLORIDA

The Florida Bar
The Florida Bar Center
650 Apalachee Parkway
Tallahassee, FL 32399-2300
(904) 561-5600

GEORGIA

State Bar of Georgia
800 The Hurt Building
50 Hurt Plaza
Atlanta, GA 30303
(404) 527-8700

*http://www.kuesterlaw.com/
comp.html*

HAWAII

Hawaii State Bar Association
1136 Union Mall
Penthouse 1
Honolulu, HI 96813
(808) 537-1868

http://www.hsba.org

IDAHO

Idaho State Bar
PO Box 895
Boise, ID 83701
(208) 334-4500

ILLINOIS

Illinois State Bar Association
424 South Second Street
Springfield, IL 62701
(217) 525-1760

INDIANA

Indiana State Bar Association
230 East Ohio Street
Indianapolis, IN 46204
(317) 639-5465

http://www.iquest.net/isba

IOWA

Iowa State Bar Association
521 East Locust
Des Moines, IA 50309
(515) 243-3179

http://www.iowabar.org

KANSAS

Kansas Bar Association
1200 Harrison Street
Topeka, KS 66601
(913) 234-5696

*http://www.ink.org/public/
cybar*

KENTUCKY

Kentucky Bar Association
514 West Main Street
Frankfort, KY 40601-1883
(502) 564-3795

http://www.kybar.org

LOUISIANA

Louisiana State Bar Association
601 St. Charles Avenue
New Orleans, LA 70130
(504) 566-1600

MAINE

Maine State Bar Association
124 State Street
PO Box 788
Augusta, ME 04330
(207) 622-7523

http://www.mainebar.org

MARYLAND

Maryland State Bar Association
520 West Fayette Street
Baltimore, MD 21201
(410) 685-7878

http://www.msba.org/msba

MASSACHUSETTS

Massachusetts Bar Association
20 West Street
Boston, MA 02111
(617) 542-3602
(617) 542-9103 (lawyer referral service)

MICHIGAN

State Bar of Michigan
306 Townsend Street
Lansing, MI 48933-2083
(517) 372-9030

http://www.umich.edu/~icle

MINNESOTA

Minnesota State Bar Association
514 Nicollet Mall
Minneapolis, MN 55402
(612) 333-1183

MISSISSIPPI

The Mississippi Bar
643 No. State Street
Jackson, Mississippi 39202
(601) 948-4471

MISSOURI

The Missouri Bar
P.O. Box 119, 326 Monroe
Jefferson City, Missouri 65102
(314) 635-4128

http://www.mobar.org

MONTANA

State Bar of Montana
46 North Main
PO Box 577
Helena, MT 59624
(406) 442-7660

NEBRASKA

Nebraska State Bar Association
635 South 14th Street, 2nd floor
Lincoln, NE 68508
(402) 475-7091

*http://www.nol.org/legal/
nsba/index.html*

NEVADA

State Bar of Nevada
201 Las Vegas Blvd.
Las Vegas, NV 89101
(702) 382-2200

*http://www.dsi.org/statebar
/nevada.htm*

NEW HAMPSHIRE

New Hampshire Bar Association
112 Pleasant Street
Concord, NH 03301
(603) 224-6942

NEW JERSEY

New Jersey State Bar Association
One Constitution Square
New Brunswuck, NJ 08901-1500
(908) 249-5000

NEW MEXICO

State Bar of New Mexico
121 Tijeras Street N.E.
Albuquerque, NM 87102

mailing address:
PO Box 25883
Albuquerque, NM 87125
(505) 843-6132

NEW YORK

New York State Bar Association
One Elk Street
Albany, NY 12207
(518) 463-3200

http://www.nysba.org

NORTH CAROLINA

North Carolina State Bar
208 Fayetteville Street Mall
Raleigh, NC 27601

mailing address:
PO Box 25908
Raleigh, NC 27611
(919) 828-4620

North Carolina Bar Association
1312 Annapolis Drive
Raleigh, NC 27608

mailing address:
PO Box 12806
Raleigh, NC 27605
(919) 828-0561

http://www.barlinc.org

NORTH DAKOTA

State Bar Association of North Dakota
515 1/2 East Broadway, suite 101
Bismarck, ND 58501

mailing address:
PO Box 2136
Bismarck, ND 58502
(701) 255-1404

OHIO

Ohio State Bar Association
1700 Lake Shore Drive
Columbus, OH 43204

mailing address:
PO Box 16562
Columbus, OH 43216-6562
(614) 487-2050

OKLAHOMA

Oklahoma Bar Association
1901 North Lincoln
Oklahoma City, OK 73105
(405) 524-2365

OREGON

Oregon State Bar
5200 S.W. Meadows Road
PO Box 1689
Lake Oswego, OR 97035-0889
(503) 620-0222

PENNSYLVANIA

Pennsylvannia Bar Association
100 South Street
PO Box 186
Harrisburg, PA 17108
(717) 238-6715

Pennsylvania Bar Institute
http://www.pbi.org

PUERTO RICO

Puerto Rico Bar Association
PO Box 1900
San Juan, Puerto Rico 00903
(809) 721-3358

RHODE ISLAND

Rhode Island Bar Association
115 Cedar Street
Providence, RI 02903
(401) 421-5740

SOUTH CAROLINA

South Carolina Bar
950 Taylor Street
PO Box 608
Columbia, SC 29202
(803) 799-6653

http://www.scbar.org

SOUTH DAKOTA

State Bar of South Dakota
222 East Capitol
Pierre, SD 57501
(605) 224-7554

TENNESSEE

Tennessee Bar Assn
3622 West End Avenue
Nashville, TN 37205
(615) 383-7421

http://www.tba.org

TEXAS

State Bar of Texas
1414 Colorado
PO Box 12487
Austin, TX 78711
(512) 463-1463

UTAH

Utah State Bar
645 South 200 East, Suite 310
Salt Lake City, UT 84111
(801) 531-9077

VERMONT

Vermont Bar Association
PO Box 100
Montpelier, VT 05601
(802) 223-2020

VIRGINIA

Virginia State Bar
707 East Main Street, suite 1500
Richmond, VA 23219-0501
(804) 775-0500

Virginia Bar Association
701 East Franklin St., Suite 1120
Richmond, VA 23219
(804) 644-0041

VIRGIN ISLANDS

Virgin Islands Bar Association
P.O. Box 4108
Christiansted, Virgin Islands
00822
(809) 778-7497

WASHINGTON

Washington State Bar
Association
500 Westin Street
2001 Sixth Avenue
Seattle, WA 98121-2599
(206) 727-8200

http://www.wsba.org

WEST VIRGINIA

West Virginia State Bar
2006 Kanawha Blvd. East
Charleston, WV 25311
(304) 558-2456

http://www.wvbar.org

West Virginia Bar Association
904 Security Building
100 Capitol Street
Charleston, WV 25301
(304) 342-1474

WISCONSIN

State Bar of Wisconsin
402 West Wilson Street
Madison, WI 53703
(608) 257-3838

http://www.wisbar.org/
home.htm

WYOMING

Wyoming State Bar
500 Randall Avenue
Cheyenne, WY 82001
PO Box 109
Cheyenne, WY 82003
(307) 632-9061

How to save on attorney fees

How to save on attorney fees

Millions of Americans know they need legal protection, whether it's to get agreements in writing, protect themselves from lawsuits, or document business transactions. But too often these basic but important legal matters are neglected because of something else millions of Americans know: legal services are expensive.

They don't have to be. In response to the demand for affordable legal protection and services, there are now specialized clinics that process simple documents. Paralegals help people prepare legal claims on a freelance basis. People find they can handle their own legal affairs with do-it-yourself legal guides and kits. Indeed, this book is a part of this growing trend.

When are these alternatives to a lawyer appropriate? If you hire an attorney, how can you make sure you're getting good advice for a reasonable fee? Most importantly, do you know how to lower your legal expenses?

When there is no alternative

Make no mistake: serious legal matters require a lawyer. The tips in this book can help you reduce your legal fees, but there is no alternative to good professional legal services in certain circumstances:

- when you are charged with a felony, you are a repeat offender, or jail is possible

- when a substantial amount of money or property is at stake in a lawsuit

- when you are a party in an adversarial divorce or custody case

- when you are an alien facing deportation

- when you are the plaintiff in a personal injury suit that involves large sums of money

- when you're involved in very important transactions

Are you sure you want to take it to court?

Consider the following questions before you pursue legal action:

What are your financial resources?

Money buys experienced attorneys, and experience wins over first-year lawyers and public defenders. Even with a strong case, you may save money by not going to court. Yes, people win millions in court. But for every big winner there are ten plaintiffs who either lose or win so little that litigation wasn't worth their effort.

Do you have the time and energy for a trial?

Courts are overbooked, and by the time your case is heard your initial zeal may have grown cold. If you can, make a reasonable settlement out of court. On personal matters, like a divorce or custody case, consider the emotional toll on all parties. Any legal case will affect you in some way. You will need time away from work. A newsworthy case may bring press coverage. Your loved ones, too, may face publicity. There is usually good reason to settle most cases quickly, quietly, and economically.

How can you settle disputes without litigation?

Consider *mediation*. In mediation, each party pays half the mediator's fee and, together, they attempt to work out a compromise informally. *Binding arbitration* is another alternative. For a small fee, a trained specialist serves as judge, hears both sides, and hands down a ruling that both parties have agreed to accept.

So you need an attorney

Having done your best to avoid litigation, if you still find yourself headed for court, you will need an attorney. To get the right attorney at a reasonable cost, be guided by these four questions:

What type of case is it?

You don't seek a foot doctor for a toothache. Find an attorney experienced in your type of legal problem. If you can get recommendations from clients who have recently won similar cases, do so.

Where will the trial be held?

You want a lawyer familiar with that court system and one who knows the court personnel and the local protocol—which can vary from one locality to another.

Should you hire a large or small firm?

Hiring a senior partner at a large and prestigious law firm sounds reassuring, but chances are the actual work will be handled by associates—at high rates. Small firms may give your case more attention but, with fewer resources, take longer to get the work done.

What can you afford?

Hire an attorney you can afford, of course, but know what a fee quote includes. High fees may reflect a firm's luxurious offices, high-paid staff and unmonitored expenses, while low estimates may mean "unexpected" costs later. Ask for a written estimate of all costs and anticipated expenses.

How to find a good lawyer

Whether you need an attorney quickly or you're simply open to future possibilities, here are seven nontraditional methods for finding your lawyer:

1) **Word of mouth**: Successful lawyers develop reputations. Your friends, business associates and other professionals are potential referral sources. But beware of hiring a friend. Keep the client-attorney relationship strictly business.

2) **Directories**: The Yellow Pages and the Martin-Hubbell Lawyer Directory (in your local library) can help you locate a lawyer with the right education, background and expertise for your case.

3) **Databases**: A paralegal should be able to run a quick computer search of local attorneys for you using the Westlaw or Lexis database.

4) **State bar associations**: Bar associations are listed in phone books. Along with lawyer referrals, your bar association can direct you to low-cost legal clinics or specialists in your area.

5) **Law schools**: Did you know that a legal clinic run by a law school gives law students hands-on experience? This may fit your legal needs. A third-year law student loaded with enthusiasm and a little experience might fill the bill quite inexpensively—or even for free.

6) **Advertisements**: Ads are a lawyer's business card. If a "TV attorney" seems to have a good track record with your kind of case, why not call? Just don't be swayed by the glamour of a high-profile attorney.

7) **Your own ad**: A small ad describing the qualifications and legal expertise you're seeking, placed in a local bar association journal, may get you just the lead you need.

How to hire and work with your attorney

No matter how you hear about an attorney, you must interview him or her in person. Call the office during business hours and ask to speak to the attorney directly. Then explain your case briefly and mention how you obtained the attorney's name. If the attorney sounds interested and knowledgeable, arrange for a visit.

The ten-point visit

1) Note the address. This is a good indication of the rates to expect.

2) Note the condition of the offices. File-laden desks and poorly maintained work space may indicate a poorly run firm.

3) Look for up-to-date computer equipment and an adequate complement of support personnel.

4) Note the appearance of the attorney. How will he or she impress a judge or jury?

5) Is the attorney attentive? Does the attorney take notes, ask questions, follow up on points you've mentioned?

6) Ask what schools he or she has graduated from, and feel free to check credentials with the state bar association.

7) Does the attorney have a good track record with your type of case?

8) Does he or she explain legal terms to you in plain English?

9) Are the firm's costs reasonable?

10) Will the attorney provide references?

Hiring the attorney

Having chosen your attorney, make sure all the terms are agreeable. Send letters to any other attorneys you have interviewed, thanking them for their time and interest in your case and explaining that you have retained another attorney's services.

Request a letter from your new attorney outlining your retainer agreement. The letter should list all fees you will be responsible for as well as the billing arrangement. Did you arrange to pay in installments? This should be noted in your retainer agreement.

Controlling legal costs

Legal fees and expenses can get out of control easily, but the client who is willing to put in the effort can keep legal costs manageable. Work out a budget with your attorney. Create a timeline for your case. Estimate the costs involved in each step.

Legal fees can be straightforward. Some lawyers charge a fixed rate for a specific project. Others charge contingency fees (they collect a percentage of your recovery, usually 35-50 percent if you win and nothing if you lose). But most attorneys prefer to bill by the hour. Expenses can run the gamut, with one hourly charge for taking depositions and another for making copies.

Have your attorney give you a list of charges for services rendered and an itemized monthly bill. The bill should explain the service performed, who performed the work, when the service was provided, how long it took, and how the service benefits your case.

Ample opportunity abounds in legal billing for dishonesty and greed. There is also plenty of opportunity for knowledgeable clients to cut their bills significantly if they know what to look for. Asking the right questions and setting limits on fees is smart and can save you a bundle. Don't be afraid to question legal bills. It's your case and your money!

When the bill arrives

- **Retainer fees**: You should already have a written retainer agreement. Ideally, the retainer fee applies toward case costs, and your agreement puts that in writing. Protect yourself by escrowing the retainer fee until the case has been handled to your satisfaction.

- **Office visit charges**: Track your case and all documents, correspondence, and bills. Diary all dates, deadlines and questions you want to ask your attorney during your next office visit. This keeps expensive office visits focused and productive, with more accomplished in less time. If your attorney charges less for phone consultations than office visits, reserve visits for those tasks that must be done in person.

- **Phone bills**: This is where itemized bills are essential. Who made the call, who was spoken to, what was discussed, when was the call made, and how long did it last? Question any charges that seem unnecessary or excessive (over 60 minutes).

- **Administrative costs**: Your case may involve hundreds, if not thousands, of documents: motions, affidavits, depositions, interrogatories, bills, memoranda, and letters. Are they all necessary? Understand your attorney's case strategy before paying for an endless stream of costly documents.

- **Associate and paralegal fees**: Note in your retainer agreement which staff people will have access to your file. Then you'll have an informed and efficient staff working on your case, and you'll recognize their names on your bill. Of course, your attorney should handle the important part of your case, but less costly paralegals or associates may handle routine matters more economically. Note: Some firms expect their associates to meet a quota of billable hours, although the time spent is not always warranted. Review your bill. Does the time spent make sense for the document in question? Are several staff involved in matters that should be handled by one person? Don't be afraid to ask questions. And withhold payment until you have satisfactory answers.

- **Court stenographer fees**: Depositions and court hearings require costly transcripts and stenographers. This means added expenses. Keep an eye on these costs.

- **Copying charges**: Your retainer fee should limit the number of copies made of your complete file. This is in your legal interest, because multiple files mean multiple chances others may access your confidential information. It is also in your financial interest, because copying costs can be astronomical.

- **Fax costs**: As with the phone and copier, the fax can easily run up costs. Set a limit.

- **Postage charges**: Be aware of how much it costs to send a legal document overnight, or a registered letter. Offer to pick up or deliver expensive items when it makes sense.

- **Filing fees**: Make it clear to your attorney that you want to minimize the number of court filings in your case. Watch your bill and question any filing that seems unnecessary.

- **Document production fee**: Turning over documents to your opponent is mandatory and expensive. If you're faced with reproducing boxes of documents, consider having the job done by a commercial firm rather than your attorney's office.

- **Research and investigations**: Pay only for photographs that can be used in court. Can you hire a photographer at a lower rate than what your attorney charges? Reserve that right in your retainer agreement. Database research can also be extensive and expensive; if your attorney uses Westlaw or Nexis, set limits on the research you will pay for.

- **Expert witnesses**: Question your attorney if you are expected to pay for more than a reasonable number of expert witnesses. Limit the number to what is essential to your case.

- **Technology costs**: Avoid videos, tape recordings, and graphics if you can use old-fashioned diagrams to illustrate your case.

- **Travel expenses**: Travel expenses for those connected to your case can be quite costly unless you set a maximum budget. Check all travel-related items on your bill, and make sure they are appropriate. Always question why the travel is necessary before you agree to pay for it.

- **Appeals costs**: Losing a case often means an appeal, but weigh the costs involved before you make that decision. If money is at stake, do a cost-benefit analysis to see if an appeal is financially justified.

- **Monetary damages**: Your attorney should be able to help you estimate the total damages you will have to pay if you lose a civil case. Always consider settling out of court rather than proceeding to trial when the trial costs will be high.

- **Surprise costs**: Surprise costs are so routine they're predictable. The judge may impose unexpected court orders on one or both sides, or the opposition will file an unexpected motion that increases your legal costs. Budget a few thousand dollars over what you estimate your case will cost. It usually is needed.

- **Padded expenses**: Assume your costs and expenses are legitimate. But some firms do inflate expenses—office supplies, database searches, copying, postage, phone bills—to bolster their bottom line. Request copies of bills your law firm receives from support services. If you are not the only client represented on a bill, determine those charges related to your case.

Keeping it legal without a lawyer

The best way to save legal costs is to avoid legal problems. There are hundreds of ways to decrease your chances of lawsuits and other nasty legal encounters. Most simply involve a little common sense. You can also use your own initiative to find and use the variety of self-help legal aid available to consumers.

11 situations in which you may not need a lawyer

1) **No-fault divorce**: Married couples with no children, minimal property, and no demands for alimony can take advantage of divorce mediation services. A lawyer should review your divorce agreement before you sign it, but you will have saved a fortune in attorney fees. A marital or family counselor may save a seemingly doomed marriage, or help both parties move beyond anger to a calm settlement. Either way, counseling can save you money.

2) **Wills**: Do-it-yourself wills and living trusts are ideal for people with estates of less than $600,000. Even if an attorney reviews your final documents, a will kit allows you to read the documents, ponder your bequests, fill out sample forms, and discuss your wishes with your family at your leisure, without a lawyer's meter running.

3) **Incorporating**: Incorporating a small business can be done by any business owner. Your state government office provides the forms and instructions necessary. A visit to your state office will probably be

necessary to perform a business name check. A fee of $100-$200 is usually charged for processing your Articles of Incorporation. The rest is paperwork: filling out forms correctly; holding regular, official meetings; and maintaining accurate records.

4) **Routine business transactions**: Copyrights, for example, can be applied for by asking the U.S. Copyright Office for the appropriate forms and brochures. The same is true of the U.S. Patent and Trademark Office. If your business does a great deal of document preparation and research, hire a certified paralegal rather than paying an attorney's rates. Consider mediation or binding arbitration rather than going to court for a business dispute. Hire a human resources/benefits administrator to head off disputes concerning discrimination or other employee charges.

5) **Repairing bad credit**: When money matters get out of hand, attorneys and bankruptcy should not be your first solution. Contact a credit counseling organization that will help you work out manageable payment plans so that everyone wins. It can also help you learn to manage your money better. A good company to start with is the Consumer Credit Counseling Service, 1-800-388-2227.

6) **Small Claims Court**: For legal grievances amounting to a few thousand dollars in damages, represent yourself in Small Claims Court. There is a small filing fee, forms to fill out, and several court visits necessary. If you can collect evidence, state your case in a clear and logical presentation, and come across as neat, respectful and sincere, you can succeed in Small Claims Court.

7) **Traffic Court**: Like Small Claims Court, Traffic Court may show more compassion to a defendant appearing without an attorney. If you are ticketed for a minor offense and want to take it to court, you will be asked to plead guilty or not guilty. If you plead guilty, you can ask for leniency in sentencing by presenting mitigating circumstances. Bring any witnesses who can support your story, and remember that presentation (some would call it acting ability) is as important as fact.

8) **Residential zoning petition**: If a homeowner wants to open a home business, build an addition, or make other changes that may affect his or her neighborhood, town approval is required. But you don't need a lawyer to fill out a zoning variance application, turn it in, and present your story at a public hearing. Getting local support before the hearing is the best way to assure a positive vote; contact as many neighbors as possible to reassure them that your plans won't adversely affect them or the neighborhood.

9) **Government benefit applications**: Applying for veterans' or unemployment benefits may be daunting, but the process doesn't require legal help. Apply for either immediately upon becoming eligible. Note: If your former employer contests your application for unemployment benefits and you have to defend yourself at a hearing, you may want to consider hiring an attorney.

10) **Receiving government files**: The Freedom of Information Act gives every American the right to receive copies of government information about him or her. Write a letter to the appropriate state or federal agency, noting the precise information you want. List each document in a separate paragraph. Mention the Freedom of Information Act, and state that you will pay any expenses. Close with your signature and the address the documents should be sent to. An approved request may take six months to arrive. If it is refused on the grounds that the information is classified or violates another's privacy, send a letter of appeal explaining why the released information would not endanger anyone. Enlist the support of your local state or federal representative, if possible, to smooth the approval process.

11) **Citizenship**: Arriving in the United States to work and become a citizen is a process tangled in bureaucratic red tape, but it requires more perseverance than legal assistance. Immigrants can learn how to obtain a "Green Card," under what circumstances they can work, and what the requirements of citizenship are by contacting the Immigration Services or reading a good self-help book.

Save more; it's E-Z

When it comes to saving attorneys' fees, E-Z Legal Forms is the consumer's best friend. America's largest publisher of self-help legal products offers legally valid forms for virtually every situation. E-Z Legal Kits and E-Z Legal Guides include all necessary forms with a simple-to-follow manual of instructions or a layman's book. E-Z Legal Books are a legal library of forms and documents for everyday business and personal needs. E-Z Legal Software provides those same forms on disk and CD for customized documents at the touch of the keyboard.

You can add to your legal savvy and your ability to protect yourself, your loved ones, your business and your property with a range of self-help legal titles available through E-Z Legal Forms. See the product descriptions and information at the back of this guide.

BE INFORMED – PROTECTED!

The E-Z Legal *Sexual Harassment Poster*

If you do not have a well-communicated sexual harassment policy, you are vulnerable to employee lawsuits for sexual harassment.

Give your employees the information they need and protect your company from needless harassment suits by placing this poster wherever you hang your labor law poster.

BONUS! Receive our helpful manual *How to Avoid Sexual Harassment Lawsuits* with your purchase of the Sexual Harassment Poster.

See the order form in this guide, and order yours today!

FEDERAL *&* STATE
Labor Law Posters

The Poster 15 Million Businesses Must Have This Year!

All businesses must display federal labor laws at each location, or risk fines and penalties of up to $7,000!
And changes in September and October of 1997 made all previous Federal Labor Law Posters obsolete;
so make sure you're in compliance—use ours!

State	Item#
Alabama	83801
Alaska	83802
Arizona	83803
Arkansas	83804
California	83805
Colorado	83806
Connecticut	83807
Delaware	83808
Florida	83809
Georgia	83810
Hawaii	83811
Idaho	83812
Illinois	83813
Indiana	83814
Iowa	83815
Kansas	83816
Kentucky	83817

State	Item#
Louisiana	83818
Maine	83819
Maryland	83820
Massachusetts	83821
Michigan	83822
Minnesota	83823
Mississippi	83824
Missouri	83825
Montana	83826
Nebraska	83827
Nevada	83828
New Hampshire	83829
New Jersey	83830
New Mexico	83831
New York	83832
North Carolina	83833
North Dakota	83834

State	Item#
Ohio	83835
Oklahoma	83836
Oregon	83837
Pennsylvania	83838
Rhode Island	83839
South Carolina	83840
South Dakota not available	
Tennessee	83842
Texas	83843
Utah	83844
Vermont	83845
Virginia	83846
Washington	83847
Washington, D.C.	83848
West Virginia	83849
Wisconsin	83850
Wyoming	83851

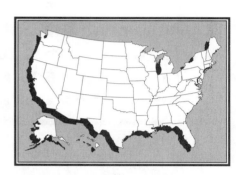

State Labor Law Compliance Poster
Avoid up to $10,000 in fines by posting the required State Labor Law Poster available from E-Z Legal.

$29.95

Federal Labor Law Poster

This colorful, durable 17³/₄" x 24" poster is in full federal compliance and includes:

- The NEW Fair Labor Standards Act Effective October 1, 1996 (New Minimum Wage Act)
- The Family & Medical Leave Act of 1993*
- The Occupational Safety and Health Protection Act of 1970
- The Equal Opportunity Act
- The Employee Polygraph Protection Act

* Businesses with fewer than 50 employees should display reverse side of poster, which excludes this act.

$11.99
Stock No. LP001

ss1999.r1

See the order form in this guide to order yours today!

E•Z Legal Kits	Item#	Qty.	Price Ea.
Bankruptcy	K100		$21.95
Incorporation	K101		$21.95
Divorce	K102		$27.95
Credit Repair	K103		$18.95
Living Trust	K105		$18.95
Living Will	K106		$21.95
Last Will & Testament	K107		$16.95
Small Claims Court	K109		$19.95
Traffic Court	K110		$19.95
Buying/Selling Your Home	K111		$18.95
Employment Law	K112		$18.95
Collecting Child Support	K115		$18.95
Limited Liability Company	K116		$18.95

★ E•Z Legal Software	Item#	Qty.	Price Ea.
Accounting-Deluxe Edition	SW1123		$49.95
Everyday Legal Forms & Agreements Made E-Z	CD311		$29.95
Managing Employees Made E-Z	CD312		$29.95
Corporate Record Keeping Made E-Z	CD314		$29.95
E-Z Construction Estimator	CD316		$29.95
Incorporation Made E-Z	SW1101		$29.95
Divorce Law Made E-Z	SW1102		$29.95
Credit Repair Made E-Z	SW1103		$29.95
Living Trusts Made E-Z	SW1105		$29.95
Last Wills Made E-Z	SW1107		$14.95
Buying/Selling Your Home Made E-Z	SW1111		$29.95
W-2 Maker	SW1117		$14.95
Asset Protection Secrets Made E-Z	SW1118		$29.95
Solving IRS Problems Made E-Z	SW1119		$29.95
Everyday Law Made E-Z	SW1120		$29.95
Vital Record Keeping Made E-Z	SW306		$29.95

★ E•Z Legal Books	Item#	Qty.	Price Ea.
Family Record Organizer	BK300		$24.95
301 Legal Forms & Agreements	BK301		$24.95
Personnel Director	BK302		$24.95
Credit Manager	BK303		$24.95
Corporate Secretary	BK304		$24.95
Immigration (English/Spanish)	BK305		$24.95
E-Z Legal Advisor	LA101		$24.95

★ Made E•Z Guides	Item#	Qty.	Price Ea.
Bankruptcy Made E-Z	G200		$17.95
Incorporation Made E-Z	G201		$17.95
Divorce Law Made E-Z	G202		$17.95
Credit Repair Made E-Z	G203		$17.95
Living Trusts Made E-Z	G205		$17.95
Living Wills Made E-Z	G206		$17.95
Last Wills Made E-Z	G207		$17.95
Small Claims Court Made E-Z	G209		$17.95
Traffic Court Made E-Z	G210		$17.95
Buying/Selling Your Home Made E-Z	G211		$17.95
Employment Law Made E-Z	G212		$17.95
Trademarks & Copyrights Made E-Z	G214		$17.95
Collecting Child Support Made E-Z	G215		$17.95
Limited Liability Companies Made E-Z	G216		$17.95
Partnerships Made E-Z	G218		$17.95
Solving IRS Problems Made E-Z	G219		$17.95
Asset Protection Secrets Made E-Z	G220		$17.95
Immigration Made E-Z	G223		$17.95
Buying/Selling a Business Made E-Z	G223		$17.95

★ Made E•Z Books	Item#	Qty.	Price Ea.
Managing Employees Made E-Z	BK308		$29.95
Corporate Record Keeping Made E-Z	BK310		$29.95
Vital Record Keeping Made E-Z	BK312		$29.95
Business Forms Made E-Z	BK313		$29.95
Collecting Unpaid Bills Made E-Z	BK309		$29.95
Everyday Law Made E-Z	BK311		$29.95
Everyday Legal Forms & Agreements Made E-Z	BK307		$29.95

★ Labor Posters	Item#	Qty.	Price Ea.
Federal Labor Law Poster	LP001		$11.99
State Labor Law Poster (specify state)			$29.95
Sexual Harassment Poster	LP003		$ 9.95
★ SHIPPING & HANDLING*			$
★ TOTAL OF ORDER**:			$

ss 1999.r1

Turn your computer into your personal lawyer

The E-Z Way to SAVE TIME and MONEY!
Print professional forms from your computer in minutes!

Everyday Legal Forms & Agreements Made E-Z
A complete library of 301 legal documents for virtually every business or personal situation—at your fingertips!
Item No. CD311 • $29.95

Credit Repair Made E-Z
Our proven formula for obtaining your credit report, removing the negative marks, and establishing "Triple A" credit!
Item No. SW1103 • $29.95

Corporate Record Keeping Made E-Z
Essential for every corporation in America. Keep records in compliance with over 170 standard minutes, notices and resolutions.
Item No. CD314 • $29.95

Divorce Law Made E-Z
Couples seeking an uncontested divorce can save costly lawyers' fees by filing the forms themselves.
Item No. SW1102 • $29.95

Incorporation Made E-Z
We provide all the information you need to protect your personal assets from business creditors...without a lawyer.
Item No. SW1101 • $29.95

Living Trusts Made E-Z
Take steps now to avoid costly, time-consuming probate and eliminate one more worry for your family by creating your own revocable living trust.
Item No. SW1105 • $29.95

Managing Employees Made E-Z
Manage employees efficiently, effectively and legally with 246 forms, letters and memos covering everything from hiring to firing.
Item No. CD312 • $29.95

Last Wills Made E-Z
Ensure your property goes to the heirs you choose. Includes Living Will and Power of Attorney for Healthcare forms for each state.
Item No. SW1107 • $14.95

ss 1999.r1

E·Z LEGAL® SOFTWARE

AS EASY AS 1,2,3!

1. Loads from 3.5" disk or CD, both included.
2. Just click on a form title to open it.
E-Z category menu and dialog box help you find the form you need.
3. Print professional forms in minutes.

Vital Record Keeping Made E-Z
Over 200 ready-to-use forms to organize every aspect of your life, from business and finance to health and recreation.
3.5 disks only.
Item No. SW306 • $29.95

Accounting–Deluxe Edition
The fastest, most economical accounting system for your small business. It handles every accounting function and is ideal for any type of business.
Item No. SW1123 • $49.95

W-2 Maker
Saves valuable time during tax season. Quickly, accurately and easily completes stacks of W-2s, W-3s, 1099s, 1096s and more. Perfect for accounting departments.
Item No. SW1147 • $14.95

Buying/Selling Your Home Made E-Z
Buy or sell almost any property with forms for listings, deeds, offers, mortgages, agreements and closing—plus helpful legal and financial tips.
Item No. SW1111 • $29.95

E-Z Construction Estimator
Every Contractor can profit from this time-saving software. It automatically calculates the detailed costs of a given project, from equipment to labor.
Item No. CD316 • $29.95

Financial Forecaster
The fast way to protect your financial future and make informed decisions. Easily calculate changes to your mortgage, investments, annuities, income and more!
Item No. SW1122 • $29.95

E·Z LEGAL® SOFTWARE

...when you need it in writing!®

E-Z Legal Software, 384 S. Military Trail, Deerfield Beach, FL 33442
(800) 822-4566 • fax: (954) 480-8906
web site: http://www.e-zlegal.com

SS 1999.r1

Microsoft, Windows, Windows NT, and the Windows logo are registered trademarks of Microsoft Corporation.

3 1170 00536 0122